Being
Beautiful

CHARTWELL
BOOKS

Helen Gordon

Illustrations by Amanda Berglund

Being Beautiful

An inspiring anthology of wit and wisdom
on what it means to be beautiful

Beauty is in the eye of the beholder.

Margaret Wolfe Hungerford

Introduction

Beauty can delight and console, inspire and excite. It can also confuse and repel, agitate and frustrate. 'It can affect us in an unlimited variety of ways,' the philosopher Roger Scruton writes. 'Yet it is never viewed with indifference: beauty demands to be noticed; it speaks to us directly like the voice of an intimate friend.'

At some level, humans appear to be hard-wired to respond to beauty. In experiments neuroscientists 'have observed that people will press a key to see an attractive face for longer, in much the same way as a mouse will press a lever to get food or drugs.' (Chelsea Ward, 'The Aesthetic Brain', *Nature*.) In Ancient Greece, Aristotle attempted to define beauty – he thought it had to do with order and symmetry – and more than 2,000 years later we're still fixated. This book, *Being Beautiful*, is a collection of quotes and extracts, wit and wisdom, which attempts to explore and celebrate human beauty in all its different forms. Contributions range from Victorian beauty manuals to twenty-first-century feminist bloggers; from poets praising the transcendent beauty of the everyday to beauty tips from actors and popstars; from the research of psychologists and neuroscientists to the work of mindfulness practitioners.

Writer and campaigner Naomi Wolf re-assesses the aging body as the body beautiful; actor Lupita Nyong'o recalls the first time she saw a black supermodel;

nineteenth-century philosopher Edmund Burke attempts to describe the perfectly beautiful eye; novelist Angela Carter interrogates the conventions of make-up. By turns joyful and thought-provoking, these and other extracts explore what 'being beautiful' might mean. Some contributors tackle the anxiety of beauty – activist Gloria Steinem writes that 'the idea that whatever I had accomplished was all about looks would remain a biased and hurtful accusation even into my old age' – while Diane Brill of Studio 54 fame celebrates the freedom for self-expression that getting dressed up affords: 'With clothes, makeup, hairstyles, you bring out different aspects of you – the you of the moment,' she writes. 'And, babe, you'd be surprised how many women you are!'

Beauty, in the extracts in this book, can be fresh-faced or made-up, old or young, found in a smile or gesture. Beauty is not just in how we look but how we act and respond to the world around us. In May 1870 the great Russian composer Tchaikovsky, who suffered all his life from periods of depression, found himself in a downbeat, contemplative mood. Worried about his health, his finances, his taxing work as a teacher at the Conservatoire, and fretting about his new opera, *Undine,* he began writing a letter, and as he did so his mood began to change: 'I am sitting at the open window (at four a.m.) and breathing the lovely air of a spring morning. . . . Life is still good . . . I assert that life is beautiful in spite of everything! . . . In a word, there are many thorns, but the roses are there too.'

Defining Beauty

1 .... Combination of qualities that delights the aesthetic senses.
2 .... [As modifier] Denoting something intended to make someone more attractive.
3 .... A beautiful woman.
4 .... An excellent example of something.
5 .... An attractive feature or advantage.

Oxford English Dictionary

Beauty
is a fat black woman
walking the fields
pressing a breezed
hibiscus
to her cheek
while the sun lights up
her feet

Beauty
is a fat black woman
riding the waves
drifting in happy oblivion
while the sea turns back
to hug her shape.

Grace Nichols

Every person has beauty at some point in their lifetime. Usually in different degrees. Sometimes they have the looks when they're a baby and they don't have it when they're grown up, but then they could get it back again when they're older. Or they might be fat but have a beautiful face. Or have bow-legs but a beautiful body. Or be the number one female beauty and have no tits. Or be the number one male beauty and have a small you-know-what.

Some people think it's easier for beauties, but actually it can work out a lot of different ways. If you're beautiful you might have a pea-brain. If you're not beautiful you might not have a pea-brain, so it depends on the pea-brain and the beauty. The size of the beauty. And the pea-brain.

I always hear myself saying, 'She's a beauty!' or 'He's a beauty!' or 'What a beauty!' but I never know what I'm talking about. I honestly don't know what beauty is, not to speak of what 'a' beauty is. So that leaves me in a strange position, because I'm noted for how much I talk about 'this one's a beauty' and 'that one's a beauty'. For a year once it was in all the magazines that my next movie was going to be *The Beauties*. The publicity for it was great, but then I could never decide who should be in it. If everybody's not a beauty, then nobody is, so I didn't want to imply that the kids in *The Beauties* were beauties but the kids in my other movies weren't so I had to back out on the basis of the title. It was all wrong.

I really don't care that much about 'Beauties'. What I really like are Talkers. To me, good talkers are beautiful because good talk is what I love. The word itself shows why I like Talkers better than Beauties, why I tape more than I film. It's not 'talkies'. Talkers are *doing* something. Beauties are *being* something. Which isn't necessarily bad, it's just that I don't know what it is they're being. It's more fun to be with people who are doing things.

When I did my self-portrait, I left all the pimples out because you always should. Pimples are a temporary condition and they don't have anything to do with what you really look like. Always omit the blemishes – they're not part of the good picture you want.

When a person is the beauty of their day, and their looks are really in style, and then the times change and tastes change, and ten years go by, if they keep exactly their same look and don't change anything and if they take care of themselves, they'll still be a beauty.

Schrafft's restaurants were the beauties of their day, and then they tried to keep up with the times and they modified and modified until they lost all their charm and were bought by a big company. But if they could just have kept their same look and style, and held on through the lean years when they weren't in style, today they'd be the best thing around. You have to hang on in periods when your style isn't popular, because if it's good, it'll come back, and you'll be a recognized beauty once again.

Andy Warhol

I died for beauty, but was scarce
Adjusted in the tomb,
When one who died for truth was lain
In an adjoining room.

He questioned softly why I failed?
'For beauty,' I replied.
'And I for truth, – the two are one;
We brethren are,' he said.

And so, as kinsmen met a-night,
We talked between the rooms.
Until the moss had reached our lips,
And covered up our names.

Emily Dickinson

A thing of beauty is a joy for ever:
Its loveliness increases; it will never
Pass into nothingness; but still will keep
A bower quiet for us, and a sleep
Full of sweet dreams, and health, and
John Keats quiet breathing.

If you retain nothing else, always remember
the most important Rule of Beauty. 'Who cares?'

Tina Fey

The word beauty has always seemed to me unsatisfactory. I have often felt there is an essential quality for which we have no word, and that therefore I am driven back on beauty, or elegance, which has the same problem. It is interesting that both these words are French, that they displaced Old English precursors. In any case, the word beauty has never seemed to me quite suited to the uses I have had to make of it, as though it were never really naturalized into my interior language, or what I might call my aesthetic experience, if that did not oblige me to use the word aesthetic. Why this awkwardness? Why must we lapse into French or Greek to speak of an experience that is surely primary and universal? Perhaps the awkwardness of the language refers to the fact that the experience of beauty is itself complex. We all know we can be conditioned to see beauty where our culture or our generation tells us to see it . . . And we know beauty can be fraudulent, compromised. Whenever power or privilege wishes to flaunt itself, it recruits beauty into its service, or something that can at least pass as beauty and will achieve the same effect. So it is entirely appropriate to regard beauty with a critical eye. But the point should be to discover an essential beauty, not to abandon the intuition altogether.

Marilynne Robinson

I shall proceed to consider the fundamental principles, which are generally allowed to give elegance and beauty, when duly blended together, to compositions of all kinds whatever; and point out to my readers, the particular force of each, in those compositions in nature and art, which seem most to *please and entertain the eye,* and give that grace and beauty, which is the subject of this enquiry. The principles I mean, are FITNESS, VARIETY, UNIFORMITY, SIMPLICITY, INTRICACY and QUANTITY; – *all which co-operate in the production of beauty, mutually correcting and restraining each other occasionally . . .*

As the foregoing principles are the very ground-work of what is to follow; we will, in order to make them the more familiar to us, just speak of them in the way they are daily put in practice, and may be seen, in every dress that is worn; and we shall find not only that ladies of fashion, but that women of every rank, who are said to dress prettily, have known their force, without considering them as principles.

I. Fitness is first considered by them, as knowing that their dresses should be useful, commodious, and fitted to their different ages; or rich, airy, and loose, agreeable to the character they would give out to the public by their dress.

II. Uniformity is chiefly complied with in dress on account of fitness, and seems to be extended not much farther than dressing both arms alike, and having the shoes of the same colour. For when any part of dress has not the excuse of fitness or propriety for its uniformity of parts, the ladies always call it *formal.*

For which reason, when they are at liberty to make what shapes they please in ornamenting their persons, those of the best taste choose the irregular as the more engaging: for example, no two patches are ever chosen of the same size, or placed at the same height; nor a single one in the middle of a feature, unless it be to hide a blemish. So a single feather, flower, or jewel is generally placed on one side of the head; or, if ever put in front, it is turned awry to avoid formality . . .

III. Variety in dress, both as to colour and form, is the constant study of the young and gay – But then,

IV. That taudriness may not destroy the proper effect of variety, simplicity is called in to restrain its superfluities, and is often very artfully made use of to set native beauty off to more advantage. I have not known any set of people, that have more excelled in this principle of simplicity, or plainness, than the Quakers.

V. Quantity, or fullness in dress, has ever been a darling principle; so that sometimes those parts of dress, which would properly admit of being extended to a great degree, have been carried into such strange excesses, that in the reign of Queen Elizabeth a law was made to put a stop to the growth of ruffs: nor is the enormous size of the hoops at present, a less sufficient proof of the extraordinary love of quantity in dress, beyond that of convenience or elegance.

VI. The beauty of intricacy lies in contriving winding shapes, such as the antique lappets belonging to the head of the sphinx, or as the modern lappet when it is brought before. Every part of dress, that will admit of the application of this principle, has an air (as it is termed) given to it thereby; and although it requires dexterity and a taste to execute these windings well, we find them daily practised with success.

This principle also recommends modesty in dress, to keep up our expectations, and not suffer them to be too soon gratified. Therefore the body and limbs should all be covered, and little more than certain hints be given of them through the clothing.

The face indeed will bear a constant view, yet always entertain and keep our curiosity awake, without the assistance either of a mask, or veil; because vast variety of changing circumstances keeps the eye and the mind in constant play, in following the numberless turns of expression it is capable of. How soon does a face that wants expression grow insipid, though it be ever so pretty? The rest of the body, not having these advantages in common with the face, would soon satiate the eye, were it to be as constantly exposed; nor would it have more effect than a marble statue. But when it is artfully clothed and decorated, the mind at every turn resumes its imaginary pursuits concerning it. Thus, if I may be allow'd a simile, the angler chooses not to see the fish he angles for, until it is fairly caught.

William Hogarth

The chief forms of beauty are order
and symmetry and definiteness, which
the mathematical sciences demonstrate
in a special degree.

Aristotle

... when [a man] puts a thing on a pedestal and calls it beautiful, he demands the same delight from others. He judges not merely for himself, but for all men, and then speaks of beauty as if it were a property of things. Thus he says that the *thing* is beautiful; and it is not as if he counts on others agreeing with him in his judgment of liking owing to his having found them in such agreement on a number of occasions, but he *demands* this agreement of them. He blames them if they judge differently, and denies them taste, which he still requires of them as something they ought to have; and to this extent it is not open to men to say: 'Every one has his own taste.' This would be equivalent to saying that there is no such thing as taste, i.e. no aesthetic judgment capable of making a rightful claim upon the assent of all men.

Immanuel Kant

Everything in any way beautiful has its beauty of itself, inherent and self-sufficient: praise is no part of it. At any rate, praise does not make anything better or worse. This applies even to the popular conception of beauty, as in material things or works of art. So does the truly beautiful need anything beyond itself? No more than law, no more than truth, no more than kindness or integrity. Which of these things derives its beauty from praise, or withers under criticism? Does an emerald lose its quality if it is not praised? And what of gold, ivory, purple, a lyre, a dagger, a flower, a bush?

Marcus Aurelius

I have a friend who's an artist and has sometimes taken a view which I don't agree with very well. He'll hold up a flower and say 'look how beautiful it is', and I'll agree. Then he says 'I as an artist can see how beautiful this is but you as a scientist take this all apart and it becomes a dull thing', and I think that he's kind of nutty. First of all, the beauty that he sees is available to other people and to me too, I believe . . .

I can appreciate the beauty of a flower. At the same time, I see much more about the flower than he sees. I could imagine the cells in there, the complicated actions inside, which also have a beauty. I mean it's not just beauty at this dimension, at one centimetre; there's also beauty at smaller dimensions, the inner structure, also the processes. The fact that the colours in the flower evolved in order to attract insects to pollinate it is interesting; it means that insects can see the colour. It adds a question: does this aesthetic sense also exist in the lower forms? Why is it aesthetic? All kinds of interesting questions which the science knowledge only adds to the excitement, the mystery and the awe of a flower. It only adds. I don't understand how it subtracts.

Richard Feynman

The Six-Letter Word: Beauty

In the language of appearance, a vague hierarchy emerges. I think of it as less of a sleek pyramid with the word *beautiful* perched on the top than as a ziggurat composed of miniature file drawers filled with caveats and exceptions, stories and histories, desires and limitations. Still, nestled there in a perch towards the top is *beautiful,* the queen bee of all the words we use to describe looks. Not everyone strives to be *beautiful* per se, but few among us actively work *against* it. Clustered around *beautiful* are nooks filled with words like *gorgeous* and slithering passageways that describe the effect on the viewer more than the object itself (*stunning, striking,* even *ravishing* – which, by the way, comes from *ravish,* i.e., *rape*) . . .

Attractive also comes in handy when describing ourselves. One of the greatest sins a woman can commit is letting other people know she's aware of her appeal, so to openly refer to oneself as *beautiful* requires chutzpah that most of us don't have. *Pretty* isn't quite as shocking to hear as a self-descriptor, but it's still in the danger zone – like *beautiful,* it goes against the cultural script we've written that allows women to claim their visual appeal only after they've qualified it. *Attractive* is a modest alternative that allows the same detached appraisal that it offers when we use it to describe others. It's tidy, neutral, and matter-of-fact, which allows us to acknowledge our own appeal without seeming vain – unless, of course, one is aware enough of language to recognize that using the word *attractive* implies that others are attracted to you. Luckily for those linguistically minded souls, the word is easily downgraded. When asking women to describe their looks, I was struck by how often they used the word pairing of *reasonably attractive*. So encoded is the need not to sound *too* pleased with our own looks that we take pains to clarify that we're only attractive *within reason . . .*

And then there's the queen bee: *beautiful*. Tolstoy may have written that 'It is amazing how complete is the delusion that beauty is goodness,' but etymologically speaking, it's not a delusion at all. The word beauty shares a Proto-Indo-European language root with *bene-*, as in *beneficial* and *benevolent*. As in *good*.

Used as concrete noun as opposed to an abstract one, *beauty* applies to women only: *She's quite a beauty.* (*He* certainly isn't.) Used as a proper noun, it can apply to both sexes, but guess which sex has a panoply of beauty terms available as a first name? In 2013, Bella was the 58th most popular baby name for girls in the United States; Beau, 270th for boys – quite a difference, even accounting for the *Twilight* effect, which saw a heroine named Bella lead a quartet of young-adult novels to the best-seller list. Not that most beauty derived names are as literal a translation as the Italian *bella* or French *beau*. A partial offering of girls' names rooted in appearance includes

Lana (Gaelic, meaning *attractive*), Belinda (Italian, *very beautiful*), Callista (Greek, *most beautiful*), Inga (Danish, *beautiful daughter*), Helen and its myriad variants (thousand ships and whatnot), Shana (Yiddish, *beautiful*), Jamille (Arabic, *beautiful*), Jolie (French, *pretty*), Leanne (Gaelic, *light, beautiful woman*), Alina (Polish, *beautiful*), Bonnie (Scottish dialect for, well, *bonny*)… Compare that with the paltry offerings of looks-oriented male names, all of which roughly translate as *handsome*, without the superlatives and specific connotations of their sister names: Hassan (Arabic), Kenneth (Celtic), Kevin (Gaelic), and a rather esoteric name sure to delight *Twilight* fans, Cullen (Celtic – and *Twilight* devotes will remember that the vampiric Edward Cullen was paired off with none other than Bella, making for a pair of beautiful creatures, not a stand-alone male).

Beauty can even be an adjective, if you're willing to forsake *Webster's* for *Cosmo*. When I started my first job in women's magazines, I was mystified by the title 'beauty editor'. I understood what happened in the fashion department, the features department, the news department – but beauty? I mean, I'd read stories about *makeup* in ladymags; was that all it was? When I finally got up the nerve to ask the beauty editor what exactly her title meant, she shrugged. 'There's no other word that puts together hair and makeup and skin care.' Fair enough,

I suppose, and it satisfied me then. But as one beauty editor put it years later when I related this to her, 'The beauty department is the only place in women's magazines where you're describing the desired *outcome*, not the process. You don't call the fashion department the 'trim and polish department' or features 'the smart department'. Beauty is presumed to be the unified goal of the magazine's readers – indeed, readers of all mainstream women's magazines – to the point that nobody thinks twice about it.

The word *beauty* in *beauty blogger* is understood by all to encompass not only hair, makeup, and skin care but the functions of noun (we blog on the entity of *beauty*), verb (*beauty* is shorthand for the process of creating the effect of beauty), and adjective (it's not *beautiful blogging*, it's *beauty blogging*). Some might decry this as sloppy language; I champion it. Language's purpose is to help us communicate, and if the morphing of any particular word helps us do that more effectively, then bring it on. Just as the six-letter word of b-e-a-u-t-y can expand to be as flexible as we need it to be, our vocabulary for physical description continues to expand, allowing us to note – if not always celebrate – the markers that make each of us notice one another.

Autumn Whitefield-Madrano

Anjan Chatterjee

Visual beauty from a neuroaesthetic point of view has to do with configurations of elements that give us pleasure. Our brains respond to these particular configurations by activating the relevant parts of our visual cortex along with relevant parts of our reward systems.

The awful thing is that beauty is mysterious as well as terrible. God and devil are fighting there and the battlefield is the heart of man.

Fyodor Dostoevsky

On the whole, the qualities of beauty, as they are merely sensible qualities, are the following: First, to be comparatively small. Secondly, to be smooth. Thirdly, to have a variety in the direction of the parts; but, fourthly, to have those parts not angular, but melted, as it were, into each other. Fifthly, to be of a delicate frame, without any remarkable appearance of strength. Sixthly, to have its colours clear and bright, but not very strong and glaring. Seventhly, or if it should have any glaring colour, to have it diversified with others. These are, I believe, the properties on which beauty depends; properties that operate by nature, and are less liable to be altered by caprice, or confounded by a diversity of tastes, than any other.

I would warn you that I do not attribute to nature either beauty or deformity, order or confusion. Only in relation to our imagination can things be called beautiful or ugly, well-ordered or confused.

Baruch Spinoza

George Santayana We have now reached our definition of beauty, which, in the terms of our successive analysis and narrowing of the conception, is value positive, intrinsic, and objectified. Or, in less technical language, Beauty is pleasure regarded as the quality of a thing.

This definition is intended to sum up a variety of distinctions and identifications which should perhaps be here more explicitly set down. Beauty is a value, that is, it is not a perception of a matter of fact or of a relation: it is an emotion, an affection of our volitional and appreciative nature.

I heard the old, old men say,
'Everything alters,
And one by one we drop away.'
They had hands like claws, and their knees
Were twisted like the old thorn-trees
By the waters.
I heard the old, old men say,
'All that's beautiful drifts away
Like the waters.'

William Butler Yeats

We must stop treating beauty as a thing
or quality, and see it instead as a kind
of communication. We often speak as if
beauty were a property of objects: Some
people or artworks 'have' it and some
do not. But *pace* Kant and Burke, the
judgement of beauty in a person or artwork
varies enormously from one person to
the next, and in the course of time, even
within the same person. These shifts and
differences are meaningful and valid,
and not 'fallings away' from some 'truth'
or 'higher taste'. Beauty is an unstable
property because it is not a property at all.
It is the name of a particular interaction
between two beings, a 'self' and an 'Other':
'I find an Other beautiful.' This act of
discovery . . . has profound implications.

Wendy Steiner

Elaine Scarry
What is the felt experience of cognition at the moment one stands in the presence of a beautiful boy or flower or bird? It seems to incite, even to require, the act of replication. Wittgenstein says that when the eye sees something beautiful, the hand wants to draw it.

Beauty brings copies of itself into being. It makes us draw it, take photographs of it, or describe it to other people. Sometimes it gives rise to exact replication and other times to resemblances and still other times to things whose connection to the original site of inspiration is unrecognizable. A beautiful face drawn by Verrocchio suddenly glides into the perceptual field of a young boy named Leonardo. The boy copies the face, then copies the face again. Then again and again and again. He does the same thing when a beautiful living plant – a violet, a wild rose – glides into his field of vision, or a living face: he makes a first copy, a second copy, a third, a fourth, a fifth. He draws it over and over, just as Pater (who tells us all this about Leonardo) replicates – now in sentences – Leonardo's acts, so that the essay reenacts its subject, becoming a sequence of faces: an angel, a Medusa, a woman and child, a Madonna, John the Baptist, St Anne, La Gioconda. Before long the means are found to replicate, thousands of times over, both the sentences and the faces, so that traces of Pater's paragraphs and Leonardo's drawings inhabit all the pockets of the world (as pieces of them float in the paragraph now before you).

A visual event may reproduce itself in the realm of touch (as when the seen face incites an ache of longing in the hand,

and the hand then presses pencil to paper), which may in turn then reappear in a second visual event, the finished drawing. This crisscrossing of the senses may happen in any direction. Wittgenstein speaks not only about beautiful visual events prompting motions in the hand but, elsewhere, about heard music that later prompts a ghostly subanatomical event in his teeth and gums. So, too, an act of touch may reproduce itself as an acoustical event or even an abstract idea, the way whenever Augustine touches something smooth, he begins to think of music and of God.

The generation is unceasing. Beauty, as both Plato's *Symposium* and everyday life confirm, prompts the begetting of children: when the eye sees someone beautiful, the whole body wants to reproduce the person. But it also – as Diotima tells Socrates – prompts the begetting of poems and laws, the works of Homer, Hesiod, and Lycurgus. The poem and the law may then prompt descriptions of themselves – literary and legal commentaries – that seek to make the beauty of the prior thing more evident, to make, in other words, the poem's or law's 'clear discernibility' even more 'clearly discernible'. Thus the beauty of Beatrice in *La vita nuova* requires of Dante the writing of a sonnet, and the writing of that one sonnet prompts the writing of another: 'After completing this last sonnet I was moved by a desire to write more poetry.' The sonnets, in turn, place on Dante a new pressure, for as soon as his ear hears what he has made in meter, his hand wants to draw a sketch of it in prose: 'This sonnet is divided into two parts . . .'; 'This sonnet is divided into four parts . . .'.

This phenomenon of unceasing begetting sponsors in people like Plato, Aquinas, Dante the idea of eternity, the perpetual duplicating of a moment that never stops. But it also sponsors the idea of terrestrial plenitude and distribution, the will to make 'more and more' so that there will eventually be 'enough'. Although very great cultural outcomes such as the *Iliad* or the *Mona Lisa* or the idea of distribution arise out of the requirement beauty places on us to replicate, the simplest manifestation of the phenomenon is the everyday fact of staring. The first flash of the bird incites the desire to duplicate not by translating the glimpsed image into a drawing or a poem or a photograph but simply by continuing to see her five seconds, twenty-five seconds, forty-five seconds later – as long as the bird is there to be beheld. People follow the paths of migrating birds, moving strangers, and lost manuscripts, trying to keep the thing sensorily present to them. Pater tells us that Leonardo, as though half-crazed, used to follow people around the streets of Florence once he got 'glimpses of it [beauty] in the strange eyes or hair of chance people'. Sometimes he persisted until sundown. This replication in the realm of sensation can be carried out by a single perceiver across time (one person staring at a face or listening to the unceasing song of a mockingbird) or can instead entail a brief act of perception distributed across many people. When Leonardo drew a cartoon of St Anne, for 'two days a crowd of people of all qualities passed in naive excitement through the chamber where it hung'. This impulse toward a distribution across perceivers is, as both museums and postcards verify, the most common response to beauty: 'Addis is full of blossoms. Wish you were here.' 'The nightingale sang again last night. Come here as soon as you can.'

Once upon a time in interior China (*neidi*), 'plateau redness' was a distinguishing mark of Tibetan women. I remember when I was young, during my first trip to Chengdu, standing amid the hustle and bustle of crowds on Chunxi Road, where, no matter what clothes you were wearing or whether you opened your mouth to speak, from the wisps of natural rouge upon one's face everyone could immediately identify a Tibetan girl.

Yet, today, walking through the streets and lanes of Lhasa, the majority of women are fair complexioned and kitted out in the latest fashion. Were you not to stop and chat with them, you would in fact never know that they were Tibetan. Often it is only on the faces of women coming from other Tibetan counties to Lhasa for pilgrimage and downing sheepskin garments that the dear, familiar wisps of rouge can be seen. . . .

[T]he reality is that, no matter whether we are talking about Tibetan men or women, very few actually think that plateau redness is attractive. Tibetan girls are just the same as Han girls, whose sense of beauty has been hijacked by drama series' from Hong Kong, South Korea and Japan, spending so much time pursuing the acquisition of white skin.

Across the highly developed cosmetic beauty industry and the explosive marketing of cosmetic products across Wechat, along with the growing collective consciousness about the need to protect our skin from the sun, Tibetan women are having their wishes fulfilled and continue on in a celebratory manner along the road to fair complexion.

In this era of unitary standards of beauty, many young Tibetan women chose to apply whitening products, matching it up with bright red lips, and constantly engaging in endless cycles of weight loss programs that leave them exhausted. For those few who still have the plateau redness, this culture gives way to feelings of embarrassment and insecurity around this natural look.

A report in the *Phoenix Weekly* found that ever since the first cosmetic branch opened up in Lhasa in the 1990s, the development of the cosmetic business in Tibet has been a story of unparalleled success. Indeed, cosmetics that get rid of redness and freckles have been the most popular. Apart from cosmetics, daily health care and make-up have another set of techniques that require mastering.

The author writes this piece hoping that everyone will gain a wider appreciation for the different kinds of beauty out there. Don't let plateau redness become something that is only seen in movies and pieces of art as a marker of Tibetan-ness, left with no option but to disappear within the narrow-minded desires of the general public.

It is precisely because of this roof of the world upon which we live, a plateau worth being proud of, that plateau redness is produced, a consequence of natural selection within this very environment. Because of the elevation above sea level across Qinghai, Tibet and other areas, the air is thin and dry, and there is little oxygen. As a result, the skin does not inhale enough, and so the red blood cells responsible for carrying oxygen increase. And when the difference in temperatures across the plateau is even more pronounced and ultraviolet rays radiate even more intensively, redness becomes all the more noticeable.

The plateau bestows upon us a superior physicality, stronger lungs and heart, and a bright red face. These natural gifts leave us with nothing to feel embarrassed about. Within this information explosion that characterises our present, so much is demanded, particularly of women. From being a perfect 50kg to the endless whitening brainwashing, we feel completely as though we ourselves are imperfect and are in need to change. In fact, there really is no need to live by the expectations of others.

Keeping a natural heart, and a natural appearance is also a manifestation of beauty.

Phuntsok Drolma, translated by Séagh Kehoe

Beauty is a primeval phenomenon,
which itself never makes its appearance,
but the reflection of which is visible
in a thousand different utterances of
the creative mind, and is as various as
nature herself.

Johann Wolfgang von Goethe

Beauty is a form of Genius – is higher, indeed, than Genius, as it needs no explanation. It is of the great facts of the world, like sunlight, or spring-time, or the reflection in dark waters of that silver shell we call the moon. It cannot be questioned. It has its divine right of sovereignty. It makes princes of those who have it. . . . People say sometimes that Beauty is only superficial. That may be so. But at least it is not so superficial as Thought is. To me, Beauty is the wonder of wonders. It is only shallow people who do not judge by appearances. The true mystery of the world is the visible, not the invisible.

Oscar Wilde

Let's make 2015 the year we take back our beauty. Why? Because only 4 percent of women consider themselves beautiful and it is time for us to raise that number.

In our culture, we are told that we are supposed to look a certain way in order to be beautiful. We are told that we are beautiful exactly as we are. We are shamed for caring about how we look, and shamed for not caring enough. This shit is powerful, important, and it deeply messes with our brains.

Beauty is officially a feminist issue. As women of all colours and creeds, we are the target market in a gigantic multi- billion- dollar worldwide ad campaign from an unregulated industry that preys on and profits from our deepest insecurities about our bodies. Our sense of 'beauty' has been hijacked by multinational cosmetics companies led mostly by rich white men. The time has come for us to take our beauty out of their hands and put it back where it belongs . . . in ours.

The Women's Liberation Movement did it's best to call to question the double standards and injustices imposed on women – and the people who perpetrate them. Today, I call to question the industry that presumes to decide 'what beauty is' without regard for the health and well-being of our bodies or our souls.

Roxie Jane Hunt

Beauty is something strange, don't you find?
To me it is a word without sense because
I do not know where its meaning comes from
nor where it leads to.

Pablo Picasso

And a poet said, Speak to us of Beauty.

And he answered:

Where shall you seek beauty, and how shall you find her unless she herself be your way and your guide?

And how shall you speak of her except she be the weaver of your speech?

The aggrieved and the injured say, 'Beauty is kind and gentle.

'Like a young mother half-shy of her own glory she walks among us.'

And the passionate say, 'Nay, beauty is a thing of might and dread.

'Like the tempest she shakes the earth beneath us and the sky above us.'

The tired and the weary say, 'Beauty is of soft whisperings.

'She speaks in our spirit.

'Her voice yields to our silences like a faint light that quivers in fear of the shadow.'

But the restless say, 'We have heard her shouting among the mountains,

'And with her cries came the sound of hoofs, and the beating of wings and the roaring of lions.'

At night the watchmen of the city say, 'Beauty shall rise with the dawn from the east.'

And at noontide the toilers and the wayfarers say, 'We have seen her leaning over the earth from the windows of the sunset.'

In winter say the snow-bound, 'She shall come with the spring leaping upon the hills.'

And in the summer heat the reapers say, 'We have seen her dancing with the autumn leaves, and we saw a drift of snow in her hair.'

All these things have you said of beauty.

Yet in truth you spoke not of her but of needs unsatisfied,

And beauty is not a need but an ecstasy.

It is not a mouth thirsting nor an empty hand stretched forth,

But rather a heart enflamed and a soul enchanted.

It is not the image you would see nor the song you would hear,

But rather an image you see though you close your eyes and a song you hear though you shut your ears.

It is not the sap within the furrowed bark, nor a wing attached to a claw,

But rather a garden forever in bloom and a flock of angels for ever in flight.

People of Orphalese, beauty is life when life unveils her holy face.

But you are life and you are the veil.

Beauty is eternity gazing at itself in a mirror.

But you are eternity and you are the mirror.

Khalil Gibran

47

Throughout the whole animal kingdom every young creature requires almost continual exercise, and the infancy of children, conformable to this intimation, should be passed in harmless gambols, that exercise the feet and hands, without requiring very minute direction from the head, or the constant attention of a nurse. In fact, the care necessary for self-preservation is the first natural exercise of the understanding, as little inventions to amuse the present moment unfold the imagination. But these wise designs of nature are counteracted by mistaken fondness or blind zeal. The child is not left a moment to its own direction, particularly a girl, and thus rendered dependent – dependence is called natural.

To preserve personal beauty, woman's glory! the limbs and faculties are cramped with worse than Chinese bands, and the sedentary life which they are condemned to live, whilst boys frolic in the open air, weakens the muscles and relaxes the nerves. As for Rousseau's remarks, which have since been echoed by several writers, that they have naturally, that is from their birth, independent of education, a fondness for dolls, dressing, and talking – they are so puerile as not to merit a serious refutation. That a girl, condemned to sit for hours together listening to the idle chat of weak nurses, or to attend at her mother's toilet, will endeavour to join the conversation, is, indeed, very natural; and that she will imitate her mother or aunts, and amuse herself by adorning her lifeless doll, as they do in dressing her, poor innocent babe! is undoubtedly a most natural consequence. For men of the greatest abilities have seldom had sufficient strength to rise above the surrounding atmosphere; and, if the page of genius has always been blurred by the prejudices of the age, some allowance should be made for a sex, who, like kings, always see things through a false medium. . . .

Women are everywhere in this deplorable state; for, in order to preserve their innocence, as ignorance is courteously termed, truth is hidden from them, and they are made to assume an artificial character before their faculties have acquired any strength. Taught from their infancy that beauty is woman's sceptre, the mind shapes itself to the body, and, roaming round its gilt cage, only seeks to adore its prison. Men have various employments and pursuits which engage their attention, and give a character to the opening mind; but women, confined to one, and having their thoughts constantly directed to the most insignificant part of themselves, seldom extend their views beyond the triumph of the hour. But was their understanding once emancipated from the slavery to which the pride and sensuality of man and their short-sighted desire, like that of dominion in tyrants, of present sway, has subjected them, we should probably read of their weaknesses with surprise. . . . Still I know that it will require a considerable length of time to eradicate the firmly rooted prejudices which sensualists have planted; it will also require some time to convince women that they act contrary to their real interest on an enlarged scale, when they cherish or affect weakness under the name of delicacy, and to convince the world that the poisoned source of female vices and follies, if it be necessary, in compliance with custom, to use synonymous terms in a lax sense, has been the sensual homage paid to beauty: – to beauty of features; for it has been shrewdly observed by a German writer, that a pretty woman, as an object of desire, is generally allowed to be so by men of all descriptions; whilst a fine woman, who inspires more sublime emotions by displaying intellectual beauty, may be overlooked or observed with indifference, by those men who find their happiness in the gratification of their appetites.

Exuberance is Beauty.

William Blake

I think beauty can mean more than what
it was ever meant to, that it can illuminate
parts of people they didn't know they had
or deserved or even wanted. I think of the
options it gives me on an everyday basis,
the ritual and the retreat: I know there are
days I would not be here it if weren't for
a small gesture of beauty I witnessed or
did by myself. Beauty makes me question
everything around me including my own
body and what I can do with it, how I
might better take care of it, how I might
be destroying it in ways I wasn't aware of.
There is always more to know and use to find
ourselves – again and again. So while it fails,
as it does, somehow it's worth the rescue.

Arabelle Sicardi

Where Beauty was, nothing ever ran quite straight, which, no doubt, was why so many people looked on it as immoral.

John Galsworthy

Perhaps beauty is simply that which speaks to us in a way that is both powerful and powerfully irrational.
Eric Jarosinski

Voltaire   Ask a toad what is beauty. . . . He will answer that it is a female with two great round eyes coming out of her little head, a large flat mouth, a yellow belly and a brown back.

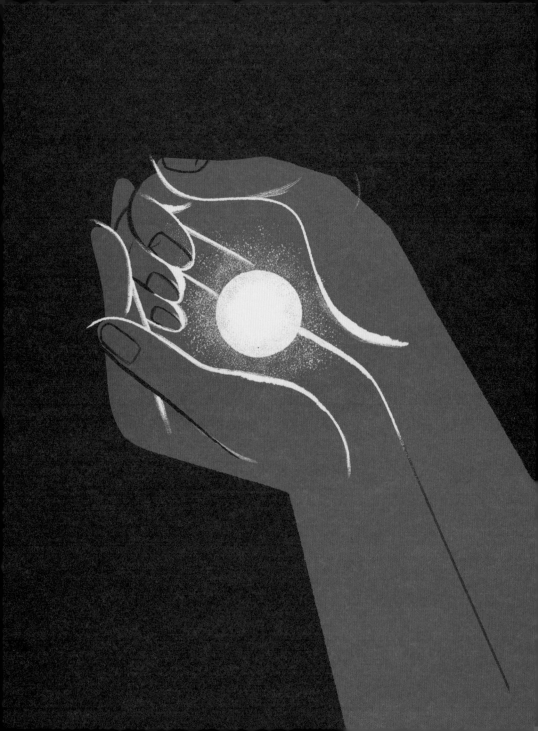

Finding Beauty

The pursuit of beauty is much more dangerous nonsense than the pursuit of truth or goodness, because it affords a greater temptation to the ego.

Northrop Frye

Do you get a lump in your throat when you see a flock of birds flying in unison? Do you feel awe and wonder when you see a massive redwood tree? Do you get a sense of love for the entire world when you find a beautiful flower in the woods? If you do, you may tend toward greater life satisfaction and well-being – and pro-environmental behaviour – than others who are connected to nature but don't experience this awe in natural beauty. Previous research has found that those of us who perceive natural beauty and are emotionally aroused by it also tend to experience greater life satisfaction and less materialism. So now we know that endorsing greater connectedness with nature and engaging with natural beauty are both associated with greater psychological well-being and environmental conservation.

Paige Brown Jarreau

Unexpected intrusions of beauty. This is what life is.

Saul Bellow

Steve Biko When you say 'black is beautiful', what in fact you are saying to him is: man, you are okay as you are, begin to look upon your self as a human being.

The first question I ask myself when something doesn't seem to be beautiful is why do I think it's not beautiful. And very shortly you discover that there is no reason.

John Cage

My mistress' eyes are nothing like the sun;
Coral is far more red than her lips' red;
If snow be white, why then her breasts are dun;
If hairs be wires, black wires grow on her head.
I have seen roses damasked, red and white,
But no such roses see I in her cheeks;
And in some perfumes is there more delight
Than in the breath that from my mistress reeks.
I love to hear her speak, yet well I know
That music hath a far more pleasing sound;
I grant I never saw a goddess go;
My mistress when she walks treads on the ground.
And yet, by heaven, I think my love as rare
As any she belied with false compare.

William Shakespeare

[Alek Wek was] a celebrated model, she was dark as night, she was on all of the runways and in every magazine, and everyone was talking about how beautiful she was. Even Oprah called her beautiful and that made it a fact. My complexion had always been an obstacle to overcome and all of a sudden Oprah was telling me it wasn't. It was perplexing and I wanted to reject it because I had begun to enjoy the seduction of inadequacy. But a flower couldn't help but bloom inside of me. When I saw Alek, I inadvertently saw a reflection of myself that I could not deny. Now, I had a spring in my step because I felt more seen, more appreciated by the far away gatekeepers of beauty.

Lupita Nyong'o

With the arrogance of
youth, I determined to do no
less than to transform the
world with Beauty. If I have
succeeded in some small way,
if only in one small corner
of the world, amongst the
men and women I love, then
I shall count myself blessed,
and blessed, and blessed, and
William Morris   the work goes on.

Hafsa Issa-Salwe

I like to think I'm providing an accurate depiction of how most children of immigrants feel when I say that we're caught up in a paradoxical nostalgia for a home that has never been. Despite my parents having yet to take me to the country that birthed them, Somalia, in my mother's case her homeland has stayed within her wherever in the world she has lived. It's evident in the food she cooks, the clothes she wears on special occasions, right down to her beauty rituals. Through her I know where I come from.

Growing up, my mother sporting bright coloured masks made from powdered *sidr* leaves or turmeric was as common a sight as rain in London. So was being her attentive servant by fetching the remote control and bringing her cups of tea whilst she was rendered immobile to avoid ruining the beautiful patterns of henna developing on her feet. Whilst I watched my mother beautify herself, she'd occasionally weave in anecdotes of Somali brides being scrubbed with a paste of ghee and dates or how she had plans to set up a salon in Mogadishu but was stopped by the impending civil war. For someone like my mother who's been away from home for decades, I can see how these rituals make you feel as though you never left, but in my case these things have enabled me to make sense of my own identity and have somewhat compensated for the formative years I might've experienced had my family stayed in Somalia.

I can't help but find humour in the fact that there were many times I felt alienated by the same differences I revel in today. To illustrate, I just couldn't understand why my mother's nails were stained with bright red henna instead of her talons being a glossy red like the manicures I saw on my friends' mothers. Interestingly enough, I'm now the first to queue up to have my henna done in preparation for a family wedding or when I return home from a holiday as is the custom in my culture. I've even incorporated henna into my haircare, but in true hybrid British and Somali style I've found a way to make it work for me by creating what's called a henna gloss, a moisturising conditioner treatment infused with henna.

Something else I've come to appreciate are the heady scents my mother likes to use with wild abandon. Much of my love for solid fragrance is owed to my mother who ensured I made the habit of using them daily, gifting me with a red and gold plastic jar containing a vanilla, amber and sandalwood scented balm. My other lesson in olfactory wasn't as direct, but rather I learned the importance of burning frankincense over coal or *uunsi*, a mix of sugar, resin and fragrances including rose, sandalwood, ylang-ylang and oud, by watching her hang a dress underneath the plumes of smoke to scent the garment before going out for the night or scenting her hair as it dried. As I write this from Saudi Arabia, the clothes in my suitcase are getting the same treatment in order to avoid that musty smell after a flight.

Those who consider beautifying oneself to be a vain and vacuous pursuit most likely haven't considered how it can connect them to their heritage, and that there's a fascinating historical context behind our beauty rituals. . . .

For me, the traditions of my grandmother and mother have taught me a great deal, especially that beauty allows you to engage with your homeland irrespective of distance.

Beauty is no quality in things themselves:
It exists merely in the mind which contemplates
them; and each mind perceives a different
beauty. One person may even perceive
deformity, where another is sensible of beauty;
and every individual ought to acquiesce in his
own sentiment, without pretending to regulate
those of others. To seek the real beauty, or
real deformity, is as fruitless an enquiry, as to
pretend to ascertain the real sweet or real bitter.
David Hume

Joseph Addison But there is nothing that makes its way more directly to the soul than beauty, which immediately diffuses a secret satisfaction and complacency through the imagination, and gives a finishing to any thing that is great or uncommon. The very first discovery of it strikes the mind with an inward joy, and spreads a cheerfulness and delight through all its faculties. There is not perhaps any real beauty or deformity more in one piece of matter than another, because we might have been so made, that whatsoever now appears loathsome to us might have shewn it self agreeable; but we find by experience that there are several modifications of matter, which the mind, without any previous consideration, pronounces at first sight beautiful or deformed. Thus we see that every different species of sensible creatures has its different notions of beauty, and that each of them is most affected with the beauties of its own kind. This is no where more remarkable than in birds of the same shape and proportion, where we often see the male determined in his courtship by the single grain or tincture of a feather, and never discovering any charms but in the colour of its species.

Il faut souffrir pour être belle.
[One must suffer to be beautiful.]
French proverb

. . . one day at the theatre, he was introduced to Odette de Crécy by an old friend of his own, who had spoken of her to him as a ravishing creature with whom he might very possibly come to an understanding; but had made her out to be harder of conquest than she actually was, so as to appear to be conferring a special favour by the introduction. She had struck Swann not, certainly, as being devoid of beauty, but as endowed with a style of beauty which left him indifferent, which aroused in him no desire, which gave him, indeed, a sort of physical repulsion; as one of those women of whom every man can name some, and each will name different examples, who are the converse of the type which our senses demand. To give him any pleasure her profile was too sharp, her skin too delicate, her cheek-bones too prominent, her features too tightly drawn. Her eyes were fine, but so large that they seemed to be bending beneath their own weight, strained the rest of her face and always made her appear unwell or in an ill humour. Some time after this introduction at the theatre she had written to ask Swann whether she might see his collections, which would interest her so much, she, 'an ignorant woman with a taste for beautiful things', saying that she would know him better when once she had seen him in his 'home', where she imagined him to be 'so comfortable with his tea and his books'; although she had not concealed her surprise at his being in that part of the town, which must be so depressing, and was 'not nearly smart enough for such a very smart man'. And when he allowed her to come she had said to him as she left how sorry she was to have stayed so short a time in a house into which she was so glad to have found her way at last, speaking of him as though he had meant something more to her than the rest of the people she knew, and appearing to unite their two selves with a kind of romantic bond which had made him smile. But at the time of life, tinged already with disenchantment, which Swann was approaching, when a man can content himself with being in love for the pleasure of loving without expecting too much in return, this linking of hearts, if it is no longer, as in early youth, the goal towards which love, of necessity, tends, still is bound to love by so strong an association of ideas that it may well become the cause of love if it presents itself first. In his younger days a man dreams of possessing the heart of the woman whom he loves; later, the feeling that he possesses the heart of a woman may be enough to make him fall in love with her. And 50, at an age when it would appear – since one seeks in love before everything else a subjective pleasure – that the taste for feminine beauty must play the larger part in its procreation, love may come into being, love of the most physical order, without any foundation in desire. At this time of life a man has already been wounded more than once by the darts of love; it no longer evolves by itself, obeying its own incomprehensible and fatal laws, before his passive and astonished heart. We come to its aid; we falsify it by memory and by suggestion; recognising one of its symptoms we recall and recreate the rest. Since we possess its hymn, engraved on our hearts in its entirety, there is no need of any woman to repeat the opening lines, potent with the admiration which her beauty inspires, for us to remember all that follows. And if she begin in the middle, where it sings of our existing, henceforward, for one another only, we are well enough attuned to that music to be able to take it up and follow our partner, without hesitation, at the first pause in her voice.

The human soul is hungry for beauty. . . .
When we experience the Beautiful, there is
a sense of homecoming. Some of our most
wonderful memories are beautiful places
where we felt immediately at home. We feel
most alive in the presence of the Beautiful for
it meets the needs of our soul. For a while the
strains of struggle and endurance are relieved
and our frailty is illuminated by a different
light in which we come to glimpse behind
the shudder of appearances and sure form
of things. In the experience of beauty we
awaken and surrender in the same act. Beauty
brings a sense of completion and sureness.
Without any of the usual calculation, we can
slip into the Beautiful with the same ease as
we slip into the seamless embrace of water;
something ancient within us already trusts
that this embrace will hold us.

John O'Donohue

The Hollywood star Claudette Colbert once said to me:
'If you find a look that suits you, in your thirties or forties,
then stick to it.' I think it's good advice.
Joan Collins

Cosmetic and clothing advertisers assume
everybody wants to be beautiful. Actually,
lots of people want to be ugly. It is safer.
Being beautiful forces one out into life; so
they put life away by cultivating ugliness. This
is not done consciously, of course, but is none-
the-less a major effort by a lot of frightened
people. They work at it with evident success.
Marshall McLuhan

A few times every century, a great natural beauty is born. I am not one of them. But what nature skipped, I supplied – so much so that sometimes I cannot remember what is real and what is fake. More important, neither can anyone else.

When you care about beauty, it may be all to the good if nature is not over-generous. There is no chance then of living in a mythical past or a perpetual illusion. It does not matter what you start with, try and get by on nature alone past thirty and you are finished. I feel no nostalgia – in fact, I cringe – when I see pictures of myself taken ten years ago. I look better now, at thirty-five, than at any other time in my life. I certainly do not expect an early dotage, nor should anyone nowadays.

Luciana Avedon

Your two great eyes will slay me suddenly;
Their beauty shakes me who was once serene;
Straight through my heart the wound is quick and keen.

Only your word will heal the injury
To my hurt heart, while yet the wound is clean –
Your two great eyes will slay me suddenly;
Their beauty shakes me who was once serene.

Upon my word, I tell you faithfully
Through life and after death you are my queen;
For with my death the whole truth shall be seen.
Your two great eyes will slay me suddenly;
Their beauty shakes me who was once serene;
Straight through my heart the wound is quick and keen.

Geoffrey Chaucer

By beauty the sensuous man is led to form and to thought; by beauty the spiritual man is brought back to matter and restored to the world of sense.

Friedrich Schiller

I find beauty in unusual things, like hanging your head out the window or sitting on a fire escape.

Scarlett Johansson

You could see the signs of female aging as diseased, especially if you had a vested interest in making women too see them your way. Or you could see that if a woman is healthy she lives to grow old; as she thrives, she reacts and speaks and shows emotion, and grows into her face. Lines trace her thought and radiate from the corners of her eyes after decades of laughter, closing together like fans as she smiles. You could call the lines a network of 'serious lesions', or you could see that in a precise calligraphy, thought has etched marks of concentration between her brows, and drawn across her forehead the horizontal creases of surprise, delight, compassion, and good talk. A lifetime of kissing, of speaking and weeping, shows expressively around a mouth scored like a leaf in motion. The skin loosens on her face and throat, giving her features a setting of sensual dignity; her features grow stronger as she does. She has looked around in her life and it shows. When grey and white reflect in her hair, you could call it a dirty secret or you could call it silver or moonlight. Her body fills into itself, taking on gravity like a bather breasting water, growing generous with the rest of her. The darkening under her eyes, the weight of her lids, their minute cross-hatching, reveal that what she has been part of has left in her its complexity and richness. She is darker, stronger, looser, tougher, sexier. The maturing of a woman who has continued to grow is a beautiful thing to behold.

Havelock Ellis The family only represents
one aspect, however important
an aspect, of a human being's
functions and activities. . . .
a life is beautiful and ideal, or
the reverse, only when we have
taken into our consideration
the social as well as the family
relationship.

I felt my most beautiful at my wedding. It was the most gorgeous day, with beautiful lighting and the dress was just amazing. I think it took 80 hours to hand-sew the sequins on. The whole day was just perfect.

Kate Moss

Symmetry is one influence on perceptions of attractiveness. Faces that are more symmetrical have more redundant information than faces that are less symmetrical. We tend to like anything the brain can process quickly and easily, so people find symmetry attractive in faces.

Larissa Vingilis-Jaremko

The invention of the printing press in the fifteenth century enabled the wider diffusion of beauty remedies. One of the most influential documenters of such knowledge was Caterina Sforza, Countess of Forlì, a powerful Renaissance noblewoman who dabbled in alchemy. Between 1492 and 1509 she wrote *Gli Experimenti*, a veritable beauty manual for Renaissance women. They were urged to boil snakeskin in wine to regenerate their complexions, while an infusion of snails and mallow was said to aid hair growth. To lighten hair, ingredients such as saffron, sulphur and cinnabar were mixed into a dye. Volume 2 of *The Greenwood Encyclopaedia of Clothing through World History* (edited by Jill Condra in 2008) adds that she 'concocted several different "beauty waters" to brighten the complexion and remove freckles'. Sforza may have felt that dispensing this wisdom consolidated her image as a woman to be reckoned with, a conservator of arcane practices that were close to witchcraft.

The same source notes the existence of several similar manuscripts, such as the *Secreti* by Isabella Cortese, published in Venice in 1584. This proposes recipes 'using ingredients that nowadays appear mysterious if not scary'. For example, Cortese claimed to have discovered, during her travels in Eastern Europe, a concoction that could remove facial spots and provide the complexion of a fifteen-year-old. 'To whiten the face, it was recommended that a woman mix rosewater, rock salt, cinnamon, powdered lily bulbs, egg white and milk'; alternatively, she could try 'lemon juice, white wine, breadcrumbs and nutmeg'.

Light, clarity, the life-giving rays of the sun: as in many previous cultures, these were associated with the light of God. Thanks to its associations with youth and divinity – as well as its rarity – blonde hair was deeply desirable. To achieve it, Venetian women would soak their locks in a mixture of lemon juice, ammonia and urine, and then sit on their terraces with their hair arrayed over the wide brims of crownless straw hats (which also prevented their skins from becoming tanned). Such is the doubtful provenance of the Venetian blonde.

Lisa Ferber

There are ways people have to deal with physical beauty that they don't have to with other assets. Beautiful people are supposed to act as though they don't know they're beautiful, even if it's kind of a fact. Somebody might say, 'I'm good at math' and not apologize for it, but for a woman to say, 'Yeah, you know, I'm really pretty' – nobody does that. It's weird that people are modest about being beautiful because it's sort of an accident. But it can be a way of stepping away from being threatening, since beautiful women are seen as threats. I remember complimenting this woman who was working on a show with my then-boyfriend. I said she was really pretty and she said, 'It's amazing what a good lipstick and a great dress can do.' It made me like her more because I felt she was saying, 'I know I'm in a show with your boyfriend, but I am not a threat to you.' I felt she understood that sometimes women can be insecure about having a pretty woman around their guy, and that she could handle that with humility and manners without insulting herself.

Part of it is the social power women wield with beauty. When we say, 'Oh, that woman is so beautiful,' we give her power and mystery. Beauty simultaneously gains someone social respect and people's suspicion. Are there certain types of beauty that don't incur the wrath of other women? Or certain levels of beauty? If you work with someone who has that California-girl kind of beauty, everyone is going to want to think she's dumb, because she's pretty in that certain type of way. Whereas I think women are into someone like Angelina Jolie because she's freaky-looking but also really beautiful.

I think people believe they're supposed to apologize for beauty because it's genetic. Nobody's allowed to show that they know it, yet most of us are also raised to present ourselves confidently. If you don't groom yourself and make the effort, it looks as if you don't care – or even that you're conceited. I go through phases of not wearing makeup, and someone said to me once, 'I noticed you don't wear any makeup – how come?' I remember thinking, 'Why do I need to explain this? Is she saying that I don't have the right to think that I look good without it? Should I wear makeup just to show that I don't think I'm okay without it?'

I think as much as women are raised to believe in ourselves, we're also taught that a woman who's prettier or slimmer than the people around her will be hated – think of the whole idea of 'You're so skinny, I hate you!' That mind-set can prevent women from revealing their full bloom. It's really only been in the past few years that I've been able to not just present myself comedically, in terms of the way I look. For many years I felt like my self-presentation had to have something ridiculous about it, sort of kooky – and sure, there's always going to be an artsiness about my style. But for me to just put on a beautiful dress and feel comfortable looking elegant and serious and poised, and not have to have something ridiculous about it – I had to be ready to say, 'I can handle this.'

Artifice like art is situated in the imagination. Not only do girdle, bra, hair dyes, and makeup disguise body and face; but as soon as she is 'dressed up', the least sophisticated woman is not concerned with perception: she is like a painting, a statue, like an actor on stage, an analogon through which is suggested an absent subject who is her character but is not she. It is this confusion with an unreal object – necessary, perfect like a hero in a novel, like a portrait or a bust – that flatters her; she strives to alienate herself in it and so to appear frozen, justified to herself.

Simone de Beauvoir

A child's world is fresh and new and beautiful, full of wonder and excitement. It is our misfortune that for most of us that clear-eyed vision, that true instinct for what is beautiful and awe-inspiring, is dimmed and even lost before we reach adulthood. If I had influence with the good fairy who is supposed to preside over the christening of all children I should ask that her gift to each child in the world be a sense of wonder so indestructible that it would last throughout life, as an unfailing antidote against the boredom and disenchantments of later years, the sterile preoccupation with things that are artificial, the alienation from the sources of our strength.

Rachel Carson

How beautiful you are! You are more beautiful in anger than in repose. I don't ask you for your love; give me yourself and your hatred; give me yourself and that pretty rage; give me yourself and that enchanting scorn; it will be enough for me.

Charles Dickens

We see very little of what really goes on around us. Science is our probe into invisible realms, be it the world of the very small, of bacteria, of atoms, of elementary particles, or the world of the very large, of stars, galaxies, and even the Universe as a whole. We see these through our tools of exploration – our reality amplifiers – the telescopes, the microscopes, and the many other instruments of detection, the rod and line of the natural scientist. If we are persistent, once in a while we see Nature stir, even jump, revealing the simple beauty of the unexpected.

Marcelo Gleiser

Most people have a great desire to become fat! They are not far wrong, as extreme thinness is a much more cruel enemy to beauty than extreme stoutness. Thin people are as a rule extremely nervous and excitable by nature, they worry over trifles, and will not take life easily, all this helps to keep them thin. A good deal can be done to help them by the use of fattening foods and plenty of sleep. They should take as much sleep as they can get, rise late, go to bed early, and sleep during the day if possible.

They must lead a very regular life, take moderate exercise, do little intellectual work, and above all keep a tranquil mind. The following foods are the most fattening. Fat and juicy meats, butter, bread, cream, soups, milk, oil, potatoes, lentils, rice puddings and farinaceous foods of all kinds.

Olive oil is one of the best fatteners I know, it should be used at each meal, poured over meat or vegetables. Not only does it fatten but will keep the whole body in good order. Beer and porter are fattening but they have a bad effect on the complexion and make it muddy. It is best to drink rich red wines mixed with mineral waters which contain iron and arsenic. . . .

You may eat as many bonbons and sweet cakes as you like during the day but avoid lemon juice and acids. Remember that no food will fatten you if you persist in worrying yourself. This will also bring premature old age and wrinkles.

Beauty is often treated as an essentially feminine subject, something trivial and frivolous that women are excessively concerned with. Men, meanwhile, are typically seen as having a straightforward and uncomplicated relationship with it: they are drawn to it. The implication is that this may be unfortunate – not exactly ideal morally – but it can't be helped, because it's natural, biological. This seems more than a little ironic. Women are not only subject to a constant and exhausting and sometimes humiliating scrutiny – they are also belittled for caring about their beauty, mocked for seeking to enhance or to hold onto their good looks, while men are just, well, being men.
Adelle Waldman

For the eye has this strange property: it rests only on beauty.

Virginia Woolf

Never lose an opportunity of seeing anything beautiful, for beauty is God's handwriting.

Ralph Waldo Emerson

Imagination disposes of everything; it creates beauty,

stice, and happiness, which are everything in this world.

Blaise Pascal

Beauty can be consoling, disturbing, sacred, profane; it can be exhilarating, appealing, inspiring, chilling. It can affect us in an unlimited variety of ways. Yet it is never viewed with indifference: beauty demands to be noticed; it speaks to us directly like the voice of an intimate friend. If there are people who are indifferent to beauty, then it is surely because they do not perceive it.

Roger Scruton

We all looked like goddesses
and gods, glowing and smooth, sheathed
from head to foot by a golden essence
that glistened and refracted its aura
of power – the wonderful ichor called youth.

We moved as easily as dolphins
surging out of the ocean, cleaving
massed tons of transparent water
streaming away in swathes of bubbling
silver like the plasm of life.

Still potent from those black and white
photos, the palpable electric
charge between us, like the negative
and positive poles of a battery,
or the fingers of Adam and God.

We were beautiful, without exception.
I could hardly bear to look at those
old albums, to see the lost glamour
we never noticed when we were
first together – when we were young.

Ruth Fainlight

David McRaney

The halo effect causes one trait about a person to colour your attitude and perception of all their other traits. . . . If you like specific aspects of an individual, the halo effect causes the positive appraisal to spread to other measurements and to resist attack. Beautiful people seem more intelligent, strong people seem nobler, friendly people seem more trustworthy, and so on. When they fall short, you forgive and defend them, sometimes unconsciously.

In the last one hundred years of research, beauty seems to be the one thing that most reliably produces the halo effect. *Beauty* is shorthand, a placeholder term for an invisible mental process in which you are privy only to the final output. . . .

To see and judge a face as beautiful is to experience a tempest of brain activity informed by your culture, your experiences, and the influences of your deep evolutionary inheritance. It all adds up to an awareness that a person is or is not beautiful in a process still waiting to be unravelled. Regardless of why, people living in the same era and culture tend to agree upon standards of beauty, and those standards unconsciously influence other judgements. . . .

Unaware of the contribution of biological, psychological, and socially influenced chemical reactions inside your head, you tend to believe that what is beautiful is better than what is not in measures of worth unrelated to appearance. . . .

The tendency of the halo effect to cause physical attractiveness to colour assumptions about everything else about a person sets up two scenarios. . . . One, beautiful people don't just have the advantage of beauty, but you treat them as if they have a host of other presumed advantages that compound the advantage. And two, after years of walking through life receiving preferential treatment as though they possess the personality traits we like to see in others, beautiful people tend to believe and act as though they truly possess those attributes. Pretty people believe they are kind, smart, decent, and whatever else the halo effect produces in the eyes of their audience – whether those things are true or not.

And the true order of going, or being
led by another, to the things of love,
is to begin from the beauties of earth
and mount upwards for the sake of that
other beauty, using these steps only, and
from one going on to two, and from two
to all fair forms, and from fair forms to
fair practices, and from fair practices to
fair notions, until from fair notions he
arrives at the notion of absolute beauty,
and at last knows what the essence of
beauty is.

Plato

Alexander Pope

'Tis not a lip, or eye, we beauty call,
but the joint force and full result of all.

Living Beautifully

If you want a golden rule that will fit everybody, this is it: Have nothing in your houses that you do not know to be useful, or believe to be beautiful.

William Morris

What can you do if you are thirty
and, turning the corner of your own
street, you are overcome, suddenly, by
a feeling of bliss – absolute bliss! – as
though you'd suddenly swallowed a
bright piece of that late afternoon sun
and it burned in your bosom, sending
out a little shower of sparks into every
particle, into every finger and toe?

Katherine Mansfield

I think your whole life shows in your
face and you should be proud of that.

Lauren Bacall

Place little good perfect things around you . . . !
Their golden ripeness heals the heart.
What is perfect teaches hope.
Friedrich Nietzsche

Loss, besides provoking pangs of anger, regret and sadness, has a deadening effect on the person engulfed by it. Loss is depressing. The bereaved often doubt they can continue in a world devoid of a loved one. Enter beauty. Beauty makes the world seem worthwhile again. Plato described our stance towards beauty as erotic. We are drawn to beauty. Beauty incites ardour. It is the bridge to a sense that reality is loveable. Plato, as much as Kant, would say that beauty makes us philosophical. But for Plato this means that beauty makes us fall in love with what is perfect. I want to suggest that beauty typically, perhaps especially in times of loss, urges not stillness but renewed love of life. Beautiful elegies reflect our sense that the only fitting remembrance for one who lived is to renew life, and that our own march forward into dying is itself an affirmation of life, and in its basic character, is good.

Kathleen Marie Higgins

If someone is jealous, selfish or dishonest, they are unattractive despite their eloquence and good features. But the person who is purged of such things and is free from hatred, it is he or she who is really beautiful.

Buddha

The truth isn't always beauty but the hunger for it is.
Nadine Gordimer

I slept, and dreamed that life was Beauty;
I woke, and found that life was Duty.
Was thy dream then a shadowy lie?
Toil on, poor heart, courageously;
And thou shalt find thy dream to be
Ellen Sturgis Hooper   A noonday light and truth to thee.

I feel we understand too little about the psychology of loss to understand why the creation of beauty is so fitting as a way of marking it – why we bring flowers to the graveside, or to the funeral, or why music of a certain sort defines the mood of mourners. It is as though beauty works as a catalyst, transforming raw grief into a tranquil sadness, helping the tears to flow and, at the same time, one might say, putting the loss into a certain philosophical perspective.

Arthur Danto

The first step to take is to become aware that *love is an art*, just as living is an art; if we want to learn how to love we must proceed in the same way we have to proceed if we want to learn any other art, say music, painting, carpentry, or the art of medicine or engineering.

What are the necessary steps in learning any art?

The process of learning an art can be divided conveniently into two parts: one, the mastery of the theory; the other, the mastery of the practice. If I want to learn the art of medicine, I must first know the facts about the human body, and about various diseases. When I have all this theoretical knowledge, I am by no means competent in the art of medicine. I shall become a master in this art only after a great deal of practice, until eventually the results of my theoretical knowledge and the results of my practice are blended into one – my intuition, the essence of the mastery of any art. But, aside from learning the theory and practice, there is a third factor necessary to becoming a master in any art – the mastery of the art must be a matter of ultimate concern; there must be nothing else in the world more important than the art. This holds true for music, for medicine, for carpentry – and for love. And, maybe, here lies the answer to the question of why people in our culture try so rarely to learn this art, in spite of their obvious failures: in spite of the deep-seated craving for love, almost everything else is considered to be more important than love: success, prestige, money, power – almost all our energy is used for the learning of how to achieve these aims, and almost none to learn the art of loving.

Erich Fromm

I gave my beauty and my youth to men.
I am going to give my wisdom and
experience to animals.

Brigitte Bardot

You direct me on the path that leads to a beautiful life.
As I walk with You, the pleasures are never-ending,
and I know true joy and contentment.

Psalm 16:11

Jane Austen It would be mortifying to the feelings
of many ladies could they be made to
understand how little the heart of any man
is affected by what is costly or new in their
attire; how little it is biased by the texture
of their muslin, and how unsusceptible of
peculiar tenderness towards the spotted, the
sprigged, the mull or the jackonet. Woman is
fine for her own satisfaction alone. No man
will admire her the more, no woman like
her the better for it. Neatness and fashion
are enough for the former, and a something
of shabbiness or impropriety will be most
endearing to the latter.

The good life, we said, is a life inspired by love and guided by knowledge . . . [But] in all that differentiates between a good life and a bad one, the world is a unity, and the man who pretends to live independently is a conscious or unconscious parasite. . . .

To live a good life in the fullest sense a man must have a good education, friends, love, children (if he desires them), a sufficient income to keep him from want and grave anxiety, good health, and work which is not uninteresting. All these things, in varying degrees, depend upon the community, and are helped or hindered by political events. The good life must be lived in a good society, and is not fully possible otherwise.

Bertrand Russell

Life is abundant, and life is beautiful. And it's a good place that we're all in, you know, on this earth, if we take care of it.

Alice Walker

Beauty grows in you to the extent that love grows, because charity itself is the soul's beauty.

Augustine of Hippo

Psychological blockages are part of a much larger set of limitations: those of mortal life itself. There are only so many professions, sexual partners, houses, entertainments and amusements available; and we only have so many days to invest in each.

To commit to *this* job, *this* spouse, *this* leisure, *this* gadget is to withdraw time, energy and wherewithal from another possibility. This economy extends from the most obvious and pointed life choices to the inestimable, inarticulate decisions we make each and every hour. Put simply, to be human is to be finite – 'born to a limited situation', as Goethe put it. Because of this, the good life warrants an ongoing struggle to be clear about what's important, and to seek it with lucidity and passion; not to be distracted by false ambitions, or waylaid by dissipated consciousness. The conundrum is captured in the Latin root of the word *distraction*, meaning literally to tear apart or pull asunder. When we are distracted, we're dragged away from what's worthwhile. . . .

The implications of this are relatively simple but immensely important. At the heart of distraction is not neurophysiology but an ongoing struggle to flourish within the limitations of mortality. We have only one life, and it's marked by all sorts of deprivations, irreversibilities and entrenched habits. And we often have to negotiate these with diminishing hours and flagging potencies. For these reasons we need to be sincere and judicious in our existential commitments and prudent in our efforts to succeed in each. To be diverted isn't simply to have too many stimuli but to be confused about what to attend to and why. Distraction is the very opposite of emancipation: failing to see what is worthwhile in life, and lacking the wherewithal to seek it.

Familiar acts are beautiful through love.

Percy Bysshe Shelley

A healthy body can be a size 6 or a size 16. Embrace what you have and learn to love your perfections and imperfections equally. You are unique; there is no one else like you in the whole wide world so why try to be someone you're not!

I believe in being the best version of yourself and living up to your potential. I believe in having role models and looking up to people who inspire you. But don't compare yourself to others – I find that whenever I do this, I forget about all the things I have achieved or the things that I love about myself. The most beautiful people are those who are happy and confident within themselves, not those who try to imitate others.

Jesinta Campbell

Life shrinks or expands in proportion to one's courage.
Anaïs Nin

Caitlin Moran There's no POINT in feminism if, when the mood takes you, and/or you are in oestrus, and wish to mate, you can't slut up in some top-ranking freakum dress and absolutely grind on the dancefloor like you heard they were handing out gold medals for hotness. You're a furry mammal. This is your birthright. YOU GO GIRLFRIEND.

What is worth remembering, however, is how infrequently there's actually any point in doing all this. Being sexy takes a lot of energy – both in the preparation of the sexiness, and the dealing with the consequences of being sexy. You know what I'm talking about. The bloke at the bar who looks like the really terrible one off *The Apprentice*, who keeps doing that winking thing. Your sexiness was not meant for him! And now you have to explain that. There's an hour wasted.

I would estimate that, currently, our culture 'gets sexy' perhaps 40 per cent too much. It's only a rough calculation. But we seem to have forgotten that women have a very pleasant alternative to looking sexy, which is just 'looking friendly and comfortable and nice', and eschews all that pouting and hair-flicking and brittle sexy chat and uncomfortable shoes and skirts you have to keep pulling down over your thighs in favour of just kinda hanging out in a nice dress, with sleeves on, and maybe a cardie, and saving the thong and the Wonderbra for special occasions (I personally favour the school sports day).

You have to have a sense of pleasure and a sense of discipline to look really well. You have to have a sound, athletic body, lead a busy life, and worry less. Live correctly and take risks.

Diana Vreeland

Beauty is that quality which, next to money, is generally the most attractive to the worst kinds of men; and, therefore, it is likely to entail a great deal of trouble on the possessor.

Anne Brontë

An Office that Sparks Joy

You can clear your mind simply by discarding all unnecessary papers. Keep the desk area relatively clear. Arrange books and materials according to your own rules.

Consider adding a small ornamental plant. Don't make your office solely practical. It's important to add a playful touch precisely because it's a work space.

A Bedroom that Sparks Joy

Make your bedroom a space to recharge your batteries and refresh yourself for another day. Keep lighting soft and indirect, play relaxing music, and feature items and scents that spark joy. Wash sheets and pillow cases frequently.

A Bathroom that Sparks Joy

Why not enjoy your bathroom's delights? Bathe by candlelight and add bath salts, flowers, whatever you feel like.

Keep the tub and counters well-scrubbed. Take out only what you need and put it away when finished.

The toilet is your home's 'detox area'. It's important to keep the energy flowing through, so keep it uncluttered. Any decorations should spark joy and be arranged with flow in mind. Cleanliness is crucial. The ideal bathroom will have a fresh, natural aroma. Keep supplies like toilet paper out of sight in a basket or covered by a cloth.

Marie Kondo

We cannot say that a woman who is interested in make-up, for example, is automatically frivolous. . . . I'm a feminist and I wake up some mornings and just want to put the brightest colour on my lips and it makes me happy and it doesn't make me any less intelligent or any less intellectually curious. This is a conversation that is about misogyny; the idea that the things considered traditionally feminine have to be degraded and diminished.

I do sympathise with the history . . . I can see why women at the start of the western feminist movement decided to push back the idea that we're not pretty; that we don't want to perform femininity any more and that we want to disavow the whole package; I can understand that. But it's 2017. We can now keep the baby, the bath water, the bath tub . . . you know, we don't have to throw everything out.

Chimamanda Ngozi Adichie

The object of any obligation, in the realm of human affairs, is always the human being as such. There exists an obligation towards every human being for the sole reason that he or she is a human being, without any other condition requiring to be fulfilled, and even without any recognition of such obligation on the part of the individual concerned.

Simone Weil

I believe I know the only cure, which is to make one's centre of life inside of one's self, not selfishly or excludingly, but with a kind of unassailable serenity – to decorate one's inner house so richly that one is content there, glad to welcome anyone who wants to come and stay, but happy all the same when one is inevitably alone.

Edith Wharton

Pema Chödrön   If your mind is expansive and unfettered, you will find yourself in a more accommodating world, a place that's endlessly interesting and alive. That quality isn't inherent in the place but in your state of mind.

Life is beautiful. Really, it is. Full of beauty and illusions. Life is great. Without it, you'd be dead.

Harmony Korine

Much of a mouseburger's* life is spent achieving. Well, beauty doesn't help you *there* except as a model or an actress. . . . Also, you spend a lot of your life *alone*. Beauty can't amuse you *then*, but brainwork – reading, writing, thinking, – *can*. As for what your looks mean to others, friends and loved ones grow *used* to the way you look and care more about how much you sympathise with their life problems. Beauty can't cheer them much in a crisis; your help and understanding *can*. And you're wildly interesting to talk to even when *not* helping. It seems to me that a wildly beautiful woman can't cheer and encourage her friends as much – maybe we won't *let* her. As for being beautiful *and* brainy, I'm not sure I can handle that! Yes, I know such double-blessed paragons *do* exist . . . but I'm just saying that if I had to choose beauty or brains, I'd take brains. Every time.

*people who are not prepossessing, not pretty, don't have a particularly high IQ, a decent education, good family background or other noticeable assets.

Helen Gurley Brown

Lynne Segal As feminists we had consciously disdained the dictates of the youthful beauty culture. It was easier to do when we were young ourselves, and hence less vulnerable to being ignored as intrinsically outside its radar. Yet we still remained largely unprepared for the dismay, fears, anxiety, even for many the sudden horror, which the ageing woman can experience on looking into the mirror and seeing a face she cannot accept, yet one uncannily familiar. It is frequently the face of her own ageing mother, from whom she had often struggled to distance herself. It was, for example, another very committed feminist in the USA, the cultural studies scholar Vivian Sobchack, who proclaimed in her book *Carnal Thoughts*: 'I despair of ever being able to reconcile my overall sense of well-being, self-confidence, achievement, and pleasure in the richness of the present with the image I see in the mirror.'

Ageing effects us all, and affects us all differently, but it is women who have often reported a very specific horror of ageing. It is associated, of course, with the place of the body and fertility, in women's lives; above all, with what is seen as beauty, attractiveness, good looks, in defining the quintessentially 'feminine', however fleeting, however unattainable, this will prove. 'Beauty is always doomed', as William Burroughs declared (even if only a tiny minority of men actually kill their young 'wives', as he did, accidentally).

Nothing, in my view, quite prepares us to deal easily with this. We live in an atmosphere where youth, fitness, speed, glamour are so prized that somehow, even as we age, we must still try to remain forever young, but women, in particular, must struggle vainly to retain their youthful allure. This is what has triggered that cry of women's despair, echoing down through the ages . . .

Fears of ageing are fed almost from birth by terrifying images in myth and folktale – the hag, harridan, gorgon, witch or Medusa. Such frightening figures are not incidentally female, they are quintessentially female, seen as monstrous because of the combination of age and gender. No such symbolic resonance trails through time from the male Gods of old – despite Cronus, for instance, being depicted mythically as an old man with a sickle, who had castrated his father and would later eat five of his own children . . .

It is still apparent everywhere that our cultures of ageing are gendered. 'Growing old is mainly an ordeal of the imagination – a moral disease, a social pathology – intrinsic to which is that it affects women much more than men,' protested the well-known writer and cultural critic Susan Sontag, in 1972, in an early piece addressing 'The Double Standard of Aging'.

I thought that nothing enormously bad or
good had happened to me during my life.
All the normal things had occurred. I had lived
a completely unremarkable life. I wanted only
my home, and the love and safety of those around
me, nothing else. I knew there was no particular
reason why I was put on this earth, but here I was
and I was glad to be here, awed by the beauty of
it. It was a perfect moment.

Michael Zadoorian

Life is beautiful, as long as it consumes you. When it is rushing through you, destroying you, life is gorgeous, glorious. It's when you burn a slow fire and save fuel, that life's not worth having.

D.H. Lawrence

To love. To be loved. To never forget your own insignificance. To never get used to the unspeakable violence and the vulgar disparity of life around you. To seek joy in the saddest places. To pursue beauty to its lair. To never simplify what is complicated or complicate what is simple. To respect strength, never power. Above all, to watch. To try and understand. To never look away. And never, never to forget.

Arundhati Roy

The most beautiful makeup of a woman is passion.
But cosmetics are easier to buy.

Yves Saint Laurent

You can be gorgeous at thirty, charming at forty, and irresistible for the rest of your life.

Coco Chanel

Let life be beautiful like summer flowers
and death like autumn leaves.

Rabindranath Tagore

I am sitting at the open window (at four
a.m.) and breathing the lovely air of a
spring morning . . . life is still good, [and] it
is worth living on a May morning . . . I assert
that life is beautiful in spite of everything!
This 'everything' includes the following
items: 1. Illness; I am getting much too
stout, and my nerves are all to pieces. 2. The
Conservatoire oppresses me to extinction;
I am more and more convinced that I am
absolutely unfitted to teach the theory of
music. 3. My pecuniary situation is very
bad. 4. I am very doubtful if *Undine* will be
performed. I have heard that they are likely
to throw me over. In a word, there are many
thorns, but the roses are there too.

Peter Ilich Tchaikovsky

Albert Einstein

Mrs Barjansky wrote to me how gravely living in itself causes you suffering and how numbed you are by the indescribably painful blows that have befallen you.

And yet we should not grieve for those who have gone from us in the primes of their lives after happy and fruitful years of activity, and who have been privileged to accomplish in full measure their task in life

Something there is that can refresh and revivify older people: joy in the activities of the younger generation – a joy, to be sure, that is clouded by dark forebodings in these unsettled times. And yet, as always, the springtime sun brings forth new life, and we may rejoice because of this new life and contribute to its unfolding; and Mozart remains as beautiful and tender as he always was and always will be. There is, after all, something eternal that lies beyond the hand of fate and of all human delusions. And such eternals lie closer to an older person than to a younger one oscillating between fear and hope. For us, there remains the privilege of experiencing beauty and truth in their purest forms.

There is the bad work of pride. There is also the bad work of despair – done poorly out of the failure of hope or vision.

Despair is the too-little of responsibility, as pride is the too-much.

The shoddy work of despair, the pointless work of pride, equally betray Creation. They are wastes of life.

For despair there is no forgiveness, and for pride none. Who in loneliness can forgive?

Good work finds the way between pride and despair.

It graces with health. It heals with grace.

It preserves the given so that it remains a gift.

By it, we lose loneliness:

we clasp the hands of those who go before us, and the hands of those who come after us;

we enter the little circle of each other's arms,

and the larger circle of lovers whose hands are joined in a dance, and the larger circle of all creatures, passing in and out of life, who move also in a dance, to a music so subtle and vast that no ear hears it except in fragments.

Wendell Berry

Emerging in the fifteenth century as a reaction to the prevailing aesthetic of lavishness, ornamentation, and rich materials, wabi-sabi is the art of finding beauty in imperfection and profundity in earthiness, of revering authenticity above all. In Japan, the concept is now so deeply ingrained that it's difficult to explain to Westerners; no direct translation exists.

Broadly, wabi-sabi is everything that today's sleek, mass-produced, technology-saturated culture isn't. It's flea markets, not shopping malls; aged wood, not swank floor coverings; one single morning glory, not a dozen red roses. Wabi-sabi understands the tender, raw beauty of a grey December landscape and the aching elegance of an abandoned building or shed. It celebrates cracks and crevices and rot and all the other marks that time and weather and use leave behind. To discover wabi-sabi is to see the singular beauty in something that may first look decrepit and ugly.

Wabi-sabi reminds us that we are all transient beings on this planet – that our bodies, as well as the material world around us, are in the process of returning to dust. Nature's cycles of growth, decay, and erosion are embodied in frayed edges, rust, liver spots. Through wabi-sabi, we learn to embrace both the glory and the melancholy found in these marks of passing time.

Education is beautification of the inner world and the outer world.

Amit Ray

Examine the lives of the best and most fruitful people and peoples and ask yourselves whether a tree that is supposed to grow to a proud height can dispense with bad weather and storms; whether misfortune and external resistance, some kinds of hatred, jealousy, stubbornness, mistrust, hardness, avarice, and violence do not belong among the *favourable* conditions without which any great growth even of virtue is scarcely possible.

Friedrich Nietzsche

The test of one's decency is how much of a fight one can put up after one has stopped caring, and after one has found out that one can never please the people they wanted to please.

Willa Cather

For attractive lips, speak words of kindness.

For lovely eyes, seek out the good in people.

For a slim figure, share your food with the hungry.

For beautiful hair, let a child run his fingers through it once a day.

For poise, walk with the knowledge that you will never walk alone.

Sam Levenson

The reason death sticks so closely to life isn't biological necessity – it's envy. Life is so beautiful that death has fallen in love with it, a jealous, possessive love that grabs at what it can. But life leaps over oblivion lightly, losing only a thing or two of no importance, and gloom is but the passing shadow of a cloud.

Yann Martel

While your brain is recovering from so much pep talk, why not take a swift detour to other beautiful things that make you, you? Things that don't have anything to do with silicone, mirrors or anything else to do with our looks. If we stopped being so busy shopping for anti-ageing products, perhaps we'd have a little more time to develop our careers, dust off those rusty piano-playing skills, and work on our true friendships and family bonds . . .

What are you passionate about? Is there a degree or online course that could help you sharpen your skills and make your eyes shine with fascination as a result? Could you do with a bit of yoga – (quite possibly after that exhausting mirror talk we've just had). Or do you fancy a late night swim to calm your head? And when was the last time you had a decent champagne brunch (or beer-induced football match, depending on your style) with your favourite people? All that matters. All of that gives you confidence and helps you realize that everything you need to be happy and beautiful is already inside you. Apart from the beer, maybe. . . .

Make your friendships beautiful. That doesn't mean you should cut people off if they don't have big boobs, skinny legs or a six-pack! What it actually means is that you should work on nourishing your friendship, learning to inspire but also challenge, each other – not to mention also kicking each other's butts when you get too caught up in self-doubt again. Invest time, money and energy in the people that make you glad to be alive. Building meaningful relationships and friendships often doesn't come easy, in fact it's a lot of work. But maintaining them through the difficult times, developing a history of trust and support, and knowing about each other's worth is priceless.

Still, it's not just about your close friends. In case you feel stuck in a psychology lecture, here's a practical application: Spread the love! Tell a stranger their smile has made your day, tell your colleague they did an excellent job (instant ego boost!), tell someone you love them even if they already know, compliment someone's clothing style – because really, you'd have no clue how to pull off that onesie, right?!

We urgently need to make compassion a clear, luminous and dynamic force in our polarized world. Rooted in a principled determination to transcend selfishness, compassion can break down political, dogmatic, ideological and religious boundaries. Born of our deep interdependence, compassion is essential to human relationships and to a fulfilled humanity. It is the path to enlightenment, and indispensible to the creation of a just economy and a peaceful global community.

Karen Armstrong

Your assumptions about the lives of others are in direct relation to your naïve pomposity. Many people you believe to be rich are not rich. Many people you think have it easy worked hard for what they got. Many people who seem to be gliding right along have suffered and are suffering. Many people who appear to you to be old and stupidly saddled down with kids and cars and houses were once every bit as hip and pompous as you.

When you meet a man in the doorway of a Mexican restaurant who later kisses you while explaining that this kiss doesn't 'mean anything' because, much as he likes you, he is not interested in having a relationship with you or anyone right now, just laugh and kiss him back. Your daughter will have his sense of humour. Your son will have his eyes.

The useless days will add up to something. The shitty waitressing jobs. The hours writing in your journal. The long meandering walks. The hours reading poetry and story collections and novels and dead people's diaries and wondering about sex and God and whether you should shave under your arms or not. These things are your becoming.

One Christmas at the very beginning of your twenties when your mother gives you a warm coat that she saved for months to buy, don't look at her skeptically after she tells you she thought the coat was perfect for you. Don't hold it up and say it's longer than you like your coats to be and too puffy and possibly even too warm. Your mother will be dead by spring. That coat will be the last gift she gave you. You will regret the small thing you didn't say for the rest of your life.

Say thank you.

Life is beautiful if you are on the road to somewhere.

Orhan Pamuk

As long as I breathe I hope – as long as I breathe I shall fight for the future, that radiant future, in which man, strong and beautiful, will become master of the drifting stream of his history and will direct it towards the boundless horizons of beauty, joy and happiness! Life is beautiful. Let the future generations cleanse it of all evil, oppression and violence, and enjoy it to the full.

Leon Trotsky

Inner Beauty

Do you think, because I am poor, obscure, plain, and little, I am soulless and heartless? You think wrong! I have as much soul as you, and full as much heart! And if God had gifted me with some beauty and much wealth, I should have made it as hard for you to leave me, as it is now for me to leave you. I am not talking to you now through the medium of custom, conventionalities, nor even of mortal flesh; it is my spirit that addresses your spirit; just as if both had passed through the grave, and we stood at God's feet, equal – as we are!

Charlotte Brontë

Beloved Pan, and all ye other gods who haunt this place,
give me beauty in the inward soul; and may the outward and
inward man be at one. May I reckon the wise to be the wealthy,
and may I have such a quantity of gold as a temperate man
and he only can bear and carry. Anything more? The prayer,
I think, is enough for me.

Plato

A person who has good thoughts cannot
ever be ugly. You can have a wonky nose and
a crooked mouth and a double chin and
stick-out teeth, but if you have good thoughts
they will shine out of your face like sunbeams

Roald Dahl   and you will always look lovely.

Elizabeth Taylor   I don't think of myself as 'beautiful,'
I never have. This is partly due to
my mother. During my childhood,
when people commented on my
looks, she would turn to me and
say, 'Elizabeth, you do have very
lovely eyes, but the eyes are only a
reflection of the soul. Never forget
that the only real beauty comes
from within.' Because she had such
a strong sense of character, I never
was allowed to concentrate on
my appearance.

Virtue is like a rich stone, best plain set: and surely virtue is best in a body that is comely, though not of delicate features; and that hath rather dignity of presence, than beauty of aspect. Neither is it almost seen, that very beautiful persons are otherwise of great virtue. As if nature were rather busy not to err, than in labour to produce excellency. And therefore they prove accomplished, but not of great spirit; and study rather behaviour than virtue. But this holds not always; for Augustus Caesar, Titus Vespasianus, Philip le Bel of France, Edward the fourth of England, Alcibiades of Athens, Ismael the sophi of Persia, were all high and great spirits; and yet the most beautiful men of their times. In beauty, that of favour is more than that of colour; and that of decent and gracious motion more than that of favour. That is the best part of beauty, which a picture cannot express; no nor the first sight of the life. There is no excellent beauty, that hath not some strangeness in the proportion. A man cannot tell whether Apelles or Albert Durer were the more trifler; whereof the one would make a personage by geometrical proportions; the other, by taking the best parts out of divers faces, to make one excellent. Such personages, I think, would please nobody but the painter that made them. Not but I think a painter may make a better face than ever was; but he must do it by a kind of felicity, as a musician that maketh an excellent air in music, and not by rule. A man shall see faces, that if you examine them part by part, you shall find never a good; and yet altogether do well. If it be true, that the principal part of beauty is in decent motion, certainly, it is no marvel, though persons in years seem many times more amiable; 'pulchrorum autumnus pulcher': for no youth can be comely but by pardon, and considering the youth, as to make up the comeliness. Beauty is as summer fruits, which are easy to corrupt, and cannot last; and for the most part it makes a dissolute youth, and an age a little out of countenance; but yet certainly again, if it light well, it maketh virtue shine, and vices blush.

Polish the heart, free the six senses and let them function without obstruction, and your entire body and soul will glow.
Morihei Ueshiba

Your beauty should not come from outward adornment, such as elaborate hairstyles and the wearing of gold jewellery or fine clothes. Rather, it should be that of your inner self, the unfading beauty of a gentle and quiet spirit, which is of great worth in God's sight.

1 Peter 3:3–4

Joan Collins   Real beauty comes from confidence and from being in touch with your own body. It is natural, not narcissistic, to like and enjoy your body, and any movement that gives you sensual pleasure helps to increase your awareness of yourself. Dancing, swimming, stretching, running – all these give us the opportunity to be in touch with our own physicality. And only by appreciating our own bodies can we really enjoy other people's.

. . . a free action is a beautiful action, if the autonomy of the mind and autonomy of appearance coincide.

For this reason the highest perfection of character in a person is moral beauty brought about by the fact that *duty has become its nature.*

Friedrich Schiller

Shall I compare thee to a summer's day?
Thou art more lovely and more temperate.
Rough winds do shake the darling buds of May,
And summer's lease hath all too short a date.
Sometime too hot the eye of heaven shines,
And often is his gold complexion dimmed;
And every fair from fair sometime declines,
By chance, or nature's changing course, untrimmed;
But thy eternal summer shall not fade,
Nor lose possession of that fair thou ow'st,
Nor shall death brag thou wand'rest in his shade,
When in eternal lines to Time thou grow'st.
So long as men can breathe, or eyes can see,
So long lives this, and this gives life to thee.

William Shakespeare

I swear to God, happiness is the best make-up.

Drew Barrymore

The kind of beauty I want is the most
hard to get kind that comes from within
– strength, courage, dignity.

Ruby Dee

Ralph Waldo Emerson

The felicities of design in art, or in works of Nature, are shadows or forerunners of that beauty which reaches its perfection in the human form. All men are its lovers. Wherever it goes, it creates joy and hilarity, and everything is permitted to it. It reaches its height in woman. . . . A beautiful woman is a practical poet, taming her savage mate, planting tenderness, hope, and eloquence in all whom she approaches. Some favours of condition must go with it, since a certain serenity is essential, but we love its reproofs and superiorities. . . .

And yet – it is not beauty that inspires the deepest passion. Beauty without grace is the hook without the bait. Beauty, without expression, tires. . . .

The radiance of the human form, though sometimes astonishing, is only a burst of beauty for a few years or a few months, at the perfection of youth, and in most, rapidly declines. But we remain lovers of it, only transferring our interest to interior excellence. . . .

All high beauty has a moral element in it. . . . Gross and obscure natures, however decorated, seem impure shambles; but character gives splendour to youth, and awe to wrinkled skin and grey hairs. An adorer of truth we cannot choose but obey, and the woman who has shared with us the moral sentiment, – her locks must appear to us sublime. Thus there is a climbing scale of culture, from the first agreeable sensation which a sparkling gem or a scarlet stain affords the eye, up through fair outlines and details of the landscape, features of the human face and form, signs and tokens of thought and character in manners, up to the ineffable mysteries of the intellect.

It is going to be such an honour representing my beautiful country. Miss England is all about inner beauty as well as outer beauty and I want to be a role model to the youth and with my medical background I want to bring awareness and aid to people suffering in the world.

If a young woman is caring, intelligent and charitable and she wants to participate in a beauty contest then why not?

There is a lot of prejudice against the concept but I don't agree with those who say it's degrading. I think it's empowering. I don't think I'm letting intelligent women down by doing this and I don't think I'm feeding some sort of sexist agenda.

Carina Tyrrell

. . . the best and most beautiful things in the world cannot be seen nor even touched, but just felt in the heart.

Helen Keller

The most beautiful people we have known are those who have known defeat, known suffering, known struggle, known loss, and have found their way out of the depths. These persons have an appreciation, a sensitivity, and an understanding of life that fills them with compassion, gentleness, and a deep loving concern. Beautiful people do not just happen.

Elisabeth Kübler-Ross

As a face is reflected in water, so the heart reflects the person.
Proverbs 27:19

'Whatever comes,' she said, 'cannot alter one thing. If I am a princess in rags and tatters, I can be a princess inside. It would be easy to be a princess if I were dressed in cloth of gold, but it is a great deal more of a triumph to be one all the time when no one knows it.'

Frances Hodgson Burnett

Women need to realize that life is more than appearance and external beauty. It's about your personality and inner beauty. When your inner beauty shines through, you can glow and be truly happy. Being thin isn't always healthy, just like being heavier isn't always unhealthy. So, the next time you're concerned about fitting into your jeans, think about whether you are trying to fit into society's jeans or the ones that are right for you.

Amy Randall

Beauty for Every Woman
(1930)

Beauty of face and figure should belong to every girl. With these she makes her first impression, but real, true, lasting beauty is something deeper still. It is external beauty wedded to charm. Your face, figure, hair, and clothes will attract the first glances, but it is your charm, your poise, your self which will keep for you admiration and love.

You may think perhaps that charm is something which you either do or do not possess, and that that is the end of the matter. But such is not the case at all, as you will see if you think things over this way: you have your face, your hair, your figure, and you make the very best of them as they are. You don't try to look like a blonde if you have dark hair. You make your dark locks look beautifully sleek and shining. And so it is with yourself. In you lies the capacity for being attractive and charming, and all you need to do is to develop your self with the same care you bestow on your looks. That is charm!

I am going to take it for granted that your appearance is everything it should be; that every detail has had your attention, and that when you go out you face the world quite confidently and are not worrying all the time about things which should have been put right before you left your bedroom. For that is the secret of charm; to be able to forget such things as shiny noses and so on the moment you walk away from your mirror.

If you can do this you will be making a big step in the right direction. To begin with you will lose something which perhaps you didn't know you had – a slightly worried and preoccupied look which is fatal to making a really good first impression. Others don't know that that slight frown is caused by wondering whether your hair looks right or whether your frock isn't just a little too short. They may think that you are rather a cross sort of person in spite of the fact that you look very nice. And that is the first step towards keeping people away instead of attracting them to you by the happy, eager, and interested expression on your face.

So you see how much charm you can have if you are sure of the little things about you; you can be yourself, and it is this self, unhampered by fidgeting, worry, and preoccupation, which can be so charming.

There will be no need to cultivate a beautiful expression on your face. It will appear like magic if you are quite certain that you have done the most you can with your looks and are determined to leave it at that. You will look poised, cool, unselfconscious, and people, particularly men, will think 'there is something attractive about that girl'.

My mother died at eighty-three, of cancer, in pain, her spleen enlarged so that her body was misshapen. Is that the person I see when I think of her? Sometimes. I wish it were not. It is a true image, yet it blurs, it clouds, a truer image. It is one memory among fifty years of memories of my mother. It is the last in time. Beneath it, behind it is a deeper, complex, ever-changing image, made from imagination, hearsay, photographs, memories. I see a little red-haired child in the mountains of Colorado, a sad-faced, delicate college girl, a kind, smiling young mother, a brilliantly intellectual woman, a peerless flirt, a serious artist, a splendid cook – I see her rocking, weeding, writing, laughing – I see the turquoise bracelets on her delicate, freckled arm – I see, for a moment, all that at once, I glimpse what no mirror can reflect, the spirit flashing out across the years, beautiful.

That must be what the great artists see and paint. That must be why the tired, aged faces in Rembrandt's portraits give us such delight: they show us beauty not skin-deep but life-deep.

Ursula K. Le Guin

Mark Vernon Beauty is not a fashionable subject. Toasters and lamps are beautifully designed. Dolphins and mountains are photographed in beautiful shades of blue. Celebrities and consumers alike spend a fortune on so-called beauty products. And yet, it's not hard to detect in our culture a deep suspicion of beauty.

We're inclined to suppose its artifice is only skin deep. The beautiful branding is a treacherous ploy. The beautiful smile deceives. Haunted by images of environmental degradation and the wasteful by-products of consumerism, we fear what beauty conceals, namely death and decay. The art world, too, which once specialized in creating beauty, now appears to have largely given up on it. It's as if that which is ugly, or at least ordinary, is more authentic and real. Beauty's power has become morally suspect, too, because we know that even the worst human horrors – those of war – can be given a beautiful aura with the right lighting and cinematic tricks.

Beauty may very well imprison us as readily as it liberates us. But in discarding it utterly, we're at risk of losing an older notion – that beauty can speak to us of what is good.

Iris Murdoch is our guide here. And for this reason: she

knew that beauty must be connected to morality in order to be a constructive resource for the art of living. She didn't mean morality as in 'right or wrong', but rather morality as a kind of perception – seeing that which is true, and so desiring that which is good more precisely. That's the link: beauty's appeal is that it draws us towards that which is beautiful, and that which is beautiful can be true, though we need to discern whether its allure is false, whether it's just skin deep or whether it enables us to live at depth. Beauty awakens the desire to do that, and our values must hone and shape what our desire awakens.

From this it follows that beauty speaks so powerfully to us because it promises something we desire, perhaps happiness or insight or fulfilment. This is why we love what is beautiful, and want to commit to it, often by possessing it – though we typically don't quite know what this might entail. You commit to your beautiful lover, though can't anticipate what 30 years together will bring. That lack of certainty about what beauty is promising, coupled to the way it speaks to our probably confused loves and longings, is why we will never conclusively agree about what is beautiful. Artists, designers, philosophers, lovers will continually debate it. That's the joy of the subject and its intractable nature.

We see the beauty within and cannot say no.

Dave Eggers

Carol Morgan . . . my wish for you is for you to stop worrying about your outer beauty so much. I know the saying goes, 'Beauty fades'. But I think that's a horrible statement. I prefer 'Beauty changes'. Once beautiful, always beautiful. And once you have inner beauty, that is one thing that will never change. Instead of worrying about the wrinkles on your face or the cellulite on our thighs, think about how you can be kinder and gentler. Think about how you can leave your mark on this world in a positive way.

Because that's what REALLY matters.

[There is] beauty . . . in matters of study, in conduct and custom; briefly in soul or mind. And it is precisely here that the greater beauty lies, perceived whenever you look to the wisdom in a man and delight in it, not wasting attention on the face, which may be hideous, but passing all appearance by and catching only at the inner comeliness, the truly personal; if you are still unmoved and cannot acknowledge beauty under such conditions, then looking to your own inner being you will find no beauty to delight you and it will be futile in that state to seek the greater vision, for you will be questing it through the ugly and impure.

Plotinus

When you wake up in the morning, tell yourself: the people I deal with today will be meddling, ungrateful, arrogant, dishonest, jealous, and surly. They are like this because they can't tell good from evil. But I have seen the beauty of good, and the ugliness of evil, and have recognized that the wrongdoer has a nature related to my own – not of the same blood or birth, but of the same mind, and possessing a share of the divine. And so none of them can hurt me. No one can implicate me in ugliness. Nor can I feel angry at my relative, or hate him. We were born to work together like feet, hands, and eyes, like the two rows of teeth, upper and lower. To obstruct each other is unnatural. To feel anger at someone, to turn your back on him: these are obstructions.

Marcus Aurelius

That's how powerful you are, girl. . . .
You pretty, but pretty alone is not
what people see. You the kinda pretty,
the kinda beauty, that's like a mirror.
Men and women see themselves in you,
only now they so beautiful that they
can't bear to see you go.

Walter Mosley

It is generally a feminine eye that first detects the moral deficiencies hidden under the 'dear deceit' of beauty.
George Eliot

There is nothing in the whole world that can vie with the soul in its eagerness for beauty, or in the ready power wherewith it adopts beauty unto itself. There is nothing in the world capable of such spontaneous uplifting, of such speedy ennoblement; nothing that offers more scrupulous obedience to the pure and noble commands it receives. There is nothing in the world that yields deeper submission to the empire of a thought that is loftier than other thoughts. And on this earth of ours there are but few souls that can withstand the dominion of the soul that has suffered itself to become beautiful.

Maurice Maeterlinck

There's nothing wrong with wanting to be beautiful as long as you don't allow society's definitions to overwhelm you or make you doubt yourself.

Remember that beauty is your tool and your canvas. Still, others could use a little reminding that just because you look great, you don't want your physical appearance to dictate and distract from every interaction. . . .

Appearance is often the go-to compliment for women, which should tell you how much gender influences even our most initial judgments and perceptions. In lieu of commenting on the physical, focus your attention on attributes less associated with gender.

Here's a handy list of some examples you can try:

'I love your enthusiasm' – this shows the other person that you're reading their mood and that you're receptive to positive energy.

'You're looking vivacious today' – again, emphasis on the positive without relying on femininity. Everyone likes being told they're full of life.

'You look confident' – upbeat reinforcement with the added bonus of a self-esteem boost.

'I admire the energy you contribute' – because it's always good to be acknowledged as bringing something to the table of everyday life.

'You're so much fun to be around' – reminding them that their presence matters and is appreciated.

Any of these are likely to engage the person more than an assessment of the superficial would.

Let's face it: Even in its most flattering context, beauty is predictable. Choosing these alternate phrases conveys a more genuine interest in everything the person has to offer.

Some of us might enjoy being called beautiful, and that's perfectly fine. Beauty isn't a four letter word . . . [But] no one wants their appearance to dominate how they are perceived. Women are smart, talented, fierce, passionate individuals.

We are so much more than simply beautiful.

Erin Tatum

When someone walks into a room with their head held high, smiling, establishing eye contact and giving you a firm handshake, you will immediately find them more beautiful than someone with 'perfect' features who doesn't have that air. Interestingly, when people receive positive feedback, it makes them stand even taller and smile more, so the loop continues.

Vivian Diller

The media plays such a big role in how women measure themselves against other women, so I can be in a position where I can say beauty comes from within, we're not all perfect, and the covers of magazines are of course retouched. We do not look like that.

Kate Winslet

I think love is just another type of beauty. Superficial beauty takes a backseat when that type of beauty is at play, the one you perceive when getting to know the human behind the surface. If you know and love the entirety of a person, their face, body and soul, the outside beauty perhaps becomes less relevant and a different kind of attractiveness overshadows the rest.

I know an incredibly beautiful woman who makes heads turn in every bar. She said that beauty is passing. There'll be a day when it ceases to exist. But inner beauty is a process, inner beauty allows a constant exploring; it never ends. And this is what love is being directed at: a deep, whole beauty.

Tobias Hürter

Creating an impression of beauty is rather easier than may be imagined at first thought. The fact of being beautiful is by no means a deciding point and, as a matter of fact, it is easier for a less attractive girl to create an impression of beauty than her more fortunate sister.

For the real beauty much is expected, so much that she can never be off her guard. For the ordinarily pretty girl, and even a really plain one, an impression of beauty can be built up over a lifetime.

The first and most important point to decide is the type to which you belong. Never mind your looks, make up your mind whether you are a 'tailor-made' personality, fluffily feminine, country brogue type, smart townee, clinging, helplessly dependent (but be wise and avoid this type – it is inclined to be wearing), sporty, outdoor, or whatever it may be.

Once decided, act up that personality for all you are worth. Choose clothes to suit your type and never wear any other style at all. This is not intended to mean only one fashion – but one type. If, for instance, a tailor-made style is adopted, see that all dresses, coats, hats, etc., are of a neat, plain variety. Wear shirt blouses and ties or turnback revers. Choose plain evening dresses of a good cut and material. Adopt self-coloured materials of decided tones. Wear plain, well-set jewellery. See that handbags, shoes, gloves and umbrellas are devoid of ornamentation. It is surprising the reputation for chic that can be built up around the set following of one particular style.

The next thing to think about is deportment. Deportment used to be a great point in our Victorian grandmama's day. It was mentioned in school reports, and special attention was given to the matter in finishing schools. I think our grandmamas were very clever; they knew the value of beautiful poise and graceful carriage, even if they did not enjoy so much freedom as we possess today. A gracious presence is an invaluable asset. Cultivate the walk and movement of a person of consequence, and in time people will come to think of you as such. Not only that, but the air of confidence will become a natural habit, and away will go all fears of diffidence and shyness. Auto-suggestion is the greatest power in the world. Think you are what you wish to become, and in time, you will be. . . .

Practice coming into a room . . . if the door opens inwards, with the handle on the left as you stand facing it, take the door-knob in the right hand and open the door, swinging it wide with the arm extended. Come into the room still holding the handle, and begin to push the door shut, keeping the body facing the room and bending the arm as the door begins to close behind. As the door swings to, put the left arm behind the body, take the handle from the right hand, and shut the door. It may be necessary to take a step backwards to completely close it, but that will not detract from the entrance, provided the body is kept facing the room all the time. . . . If it is a special occasion, such as a party where you are wearing your best evening frock, pause for an instant in the doorway like a picture in its frame. Do not be more than a fraction of a second, or you will find yourself posing.

In your own home arrange the furniture, decorations and light to suit your personality. Choose colours which act as a background to your own vividness. If you are a blonde, sit with a black satin cushion behind your head; if you are a brunette, have a scarlet screen or drapery to throw up your dark colouring. Endow the particular chair in which you usually sit with your own personality. Keep a little table beside so that you may put your belongings upon it when visitors call and so avoid a cluttered up appearance. See, during the daytime, that the sunlight falls at such an angle that it brings out the lights in the hair. Put a standard lamp behind the chair so that the evening effect is the same. . . . Remember that a light placed low, so that its rays strike upon some bright or white surface, will cast a reflection upwards in the same way as the footlights of a stage. This upward lighting will dispel shadows cast from undiffused overhead illumination.

Above all, think yourself into beauty. Look for your own particular good point and build around it until it becomes a definite impression and expression of yourself. Gradually people will say 'Miss Brown – yes, I know, the girl with the beautiful hands' – or lovely eyes, or charming smile. We all of us have a beauty point somewhere, which, combined with a resolution to encourage that point, will gradually lift the 'plainest Jane' to the Princess Charming category.

Lillian Bradstock and Jane Condon (1936)

[Cleopatra's] beauty, as we are told, was in itself not altogether incomparable, nor such as to strike those who saw her; but converse with her had an irresistible charm, and her presence,combined with the persuasiveness of her discourse and the character which was somehow difused about her behaviour towards others, had something stimulating about it.

Plutarch

Above all things physical, it is more important to be beautiful on the inside – to have a big heart and an open mind and a spectacular spleen.

Ellen DeGeneres

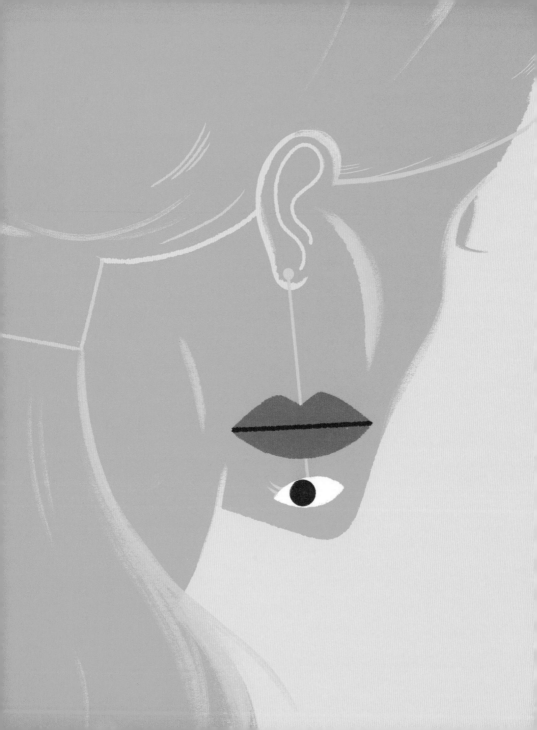

Outer Beauty

After a certain degree of prettiness,
one pretty girl is as pretty as another.

F. Scott Fitzgerald

Her pretty little upper lip, on which a delicate dark down was just perceptible, was too short for her teeth, but it lifted all the more sweetly, and was especially charming when she occasionally drew it down to meet the lower lip. As is always the case with a thoroughly attractive woman, her defect – the shortness of her upper lip and her half-open mouth – seemed to be her own special and peculiar form of beauty.

Leo Tolstoy

I had been called a 'pretty girl' before I was identified as a feminist in my mid-thirties. Then suddenly I found myself being called 'beautiful'. Not only was I described by my appearance more than ever before, but I was told that how I looked was the only reason I got any attention at all. In 1971 *The St Petersburg Times* headlined, 'Gloria's Beauty Belies Her Purpose'. It took me a few years to figure out this sudden change in response to the same person. I was being measured against the expectation that any feminist had to be unattractive in the conventional sense – and then described in contrast to that stereotype. The subtext was: *If you could get a man, why would you need equal pay?*

This grew into an accusation that I was listened to *only* because of how I looked, and a corollary that the media had created me. Though I'd been a freelance writer all my professional life without being told that my appearance was the reason I got published, it now became the explanation for everything, no matter how hard I worked. Never mind that the opposite was sometimes the case, as when my literary agent had sent me to an editor at a major national magazine, who dismissed me by saying, 'We don't want a pretty girl – we want a writer.' The idea that whatever I had accomplished was all about looks would remain a biased and hurtful accusation even into my old age.

Fortunately, travelling and speaking took me to audiences full of down-home common sense. When a reporter raised the question of my looks as more important than anything I could possibly have to say, for example, an older woman rose from the audience. 'Don't worry, honey,' she said to me comfortingly, 'it's important for someone who could play the game – and win – to say: "The game isn't worth shit."'

The French girls would tell you to believe
that you were pretty would make you so.
Elizabeth Gaskell

Beauty is all very well at first sight; but who ever looks
at it when it has been in the house three days?
George Bernard Shaw

She walks in beauty, like the night
Of cloudless climes and starry skies,
And all that's best of dark and bright
Meet in her aspect and her eyes;
Thus mellowed to that tender light
Which heaven to gaudy day denies.

Lord Byron

Appearance is the most public part of the self. It is our sacrament, the visible self that the world assumes to be a mirror of the invisible, inner self. This assumption may not be fair, and not how the best of all moral worlds would conduct itself. But that does not make it any less true. Beauty has consequences that we cannot erase by denial. Beauty will continue to operate – outside jurisdiction, in the lawless world of human attraction. Academics may ban it from intelligent discourse and snobs may sniff that beauty is trivial and shallow but in the real world the beauty myth quickly collides with reality. . . .

Although the *object* of beauty is debated, the experience of beauty is not. Beauty can stir up a snarl of emotions but pleasure must always be one (tortured longings and envy are not incompatible with pleasure). Our body responds to it viscerally and our names for beauty are synonymous with physical cataclysms and bodily obliteration – breathtaking, femme fatale, knockout, drop-dead gorgeous, bombshell, stunner, and ravishing. We experience beauty not as rational contemplation but as a response to physical urgency. . . .

We are always sizing up other people's looks: our beauty detectors never close up shop and call it a day. We notice the attractiveness of each face we see as automatically as we register whether or not they look familiar. Beauty detectors scan the environment like radar: we can see a face for a fraction of a second (150 msec. in one psychology experiment) and rate its beauty, even give it the same rating we would give it on longer inspection. Long after we forget many important details about a person, our initial response stays in our memory.

Beauty matters in economic transactions because people care about the looks of those with whom they interact. Because *people* provide services and goods, their looks become part of the goods and services that customers buy. If you buy something from a bad-looking person, you are buying a product or service whose purchase makes you less happy and less willing to pay as much. Being ugly means being less productive to your employer in many jobs. Your lower productivity results from people discriminating against you – you are harmed by the prejudices of your fellows. Consumers' preferences for beauty discriminatorily appear to make bad-looking people less productive in the eyes of their employers. But in some of these cases beauty is socially productive – it doesn't just raise sales, and perhaps profits; it also makes an arguably inherently better product or, more likely, an inherently better service.

So who causes the inferior treatment of bad-looking people in the labour markets, the discriminatorily lower earnings that they receive, the lower productivity in the minds of their employers, and the occasional fillip to the inherent quality of what we consume? We all do. As suggested by the classic comic strip, *Pogo*, 'We have met the enemy and he is us.'

Daniel S. Hamermesh

Men often tell you that the best thing for skin is making love. I cannot say I have always found the quality of their skin to be convincing evidence. The idea of therapeutic sex strikes me as rather dreary. One goes to bed with a man because of desire that may also be love, not for health and pink cheeks. I grant that no sex is a bore, but I remember a friend woefully telling me of a time when she had sex three times a day and everything, including her looks, went downhill.

Luciana Avedon

Angela Carter

At the end of [the 1960s], in a brief period of delirium, there was a startling vogue of black lipstick and red eyeshadow. For a little while we were painting ourselves up just as arbitrarily as Larionov did before the Revolution. Dada in the boudoir! What a witty parody of the whole theory of cosmetics!

The basic theory of cosmetics is that they make a woman beautiful. Or, as the advertisers say, more beautiful. You blot out your noxious wens and warts and blemishes, shade your nose to make it bigger or smaller, draw attention to your good features by bright colours, and distract from your bad features by more reticent tones. But these manic and desperate styles – leapt on and exploited instantly by desperate manufacturers – seemed to be about to break the ground for a whole new aesthetic of appearance, which would have nothing to do with the conformist ideology of 'beauty' at all. Might – ah, might – it be possible to use cosmetics to free women from the burden of having to look beautiful altogether?

Because black lipstick and red eyeshadow never 'beautified' anybody. They were the cosmetic equivalent of Duchamp's moustache on the Mona Lisa. They were cosmetics used as satire on cosmetics, on the arbitrary convention that puts blue on eyelids and pink on lips. Why not the other way round? The best part of the joke was that the look itself was utterly monstrous. It instantly converted the most beautiful women into outrageous grotesques; every face a work of anti-art. I enjoyed it very, very much.

However, it takes a helluva lot of guts to maintain oneself in a perpetual state of visual offensiveness. Most women could not resist keeping open a treacherous little corner on sex appeal. Beside, the joke went a little too near the bone. To do up your eyes so that they look like self-inflicted wounds is to wear on your face the evidence of the violence your environment inflicts on you.

Black paint around the eyes is such a familiar convention it seems natural; so does red paint on the mouth. We are so used to the bright red mouth we no longer see it as the wound it mimics, except in the treacherous lucidity of paranoia. But the shock of the red-painted eyes recalls, directly, the blinding of Gloucester in *Lear*; or, worse and more aptly, the symbolic blinding of Oedipus. Women are allowed – indeed, encouraged – to exhibit the sign of their symbolic castration – but only in the socially sanctioned place. To transpose it upwards is to allow its significance to become apparent. Scrub it off and start again. . . .

Now the mouth is back as a bloody gash, a visible wound. This mouth bleeds over everything, cups, icecream, table napkins, towels. Mary Quant has a shade called (of course) 'Bloody Mary', to ram the point home. We will leave our bloody spoor behind us to show we have been there.

Brothers Grimm

Once upon a time in the middle of winter, when the flakes of snow were falling like feathers from the sky, a queen sat at a window sewing, and the frame of the window was made of black ebony. And whilst she was sewing and looking out of the window at the snow, she pricked her finger with the needle, and three drops of blood fell upon the snow. And the red looked pretty upon the white snow, and she thought to herself, 'Would that I had a child as white as snow, as red as blood, and as black as the wood of the window-frame.'

Soon after that she had a little daughter, who was as white as snow, and as red as blood, and her hair was as black as ebony; and she was therefore called Little Snow-white. And when the child was born, the Queen died.

After a year had passed the King took to himself another wife. She was a beautiful woman, but proud and haughty, and she could not bear that anyone else chould surpass her in beauty. She had a wonderful looking-glass, and when she stood in front of it and looked at herself in it, and said,

'Looking-glass, looking-glass, on the wall,
Who in this land is the fairest of all?'

The looking-glass answered,

> 'Thou, o queen, art the fairest of all.'

Then she was satisfied, for she knew that the looking-glass spoke the truth.

But Snow-white was growing up, and grew more and more beautiful; and when she was seven years old she was as beautiful as the day, and more beautiful than the queen herself. And once when the queen asked her looking-glass,

> 'Looking-glass, looking-glass, on the wall,
> Who in this land is the fairest of all?'

It answered,

> 'Thou art fairer than all who are here, Lady Queen.
> But more beautiful still is Snow-white, as I ween.'

Then the Queen was shocked, and turned yellow and green with envy. From that hour, whenever she looked at Snow-white, her heart heaved in her breast, she hated the girl so much.

And envy and pride grew higher and higher in her heart like a weed, so that she had no peace day or night.

I didn't have any confidence in my beauty when I was young.
I felt like a character actress, and I still do.
Meryl Streep

The notion that a contemporary
woman must look mannish in order
to be taken seriously as a seeker of
Anna Wintour   power is frankly dismaying.

When I grew up, I was watching all these glamorous women with all their make-up and their pointy tits. I'd put on make-up every day of the year because I thought, 'Well, you never know who's going to knock on the door.' I ironed my hair even though my hair was pretty straight. And then I went through a period when I went to sleep with great big curlers. But you couldn't get rollers that were big enough, so we'd wash out orange juice cans and even those big tomato juice cans, and wrap our hair around that to make it sort of curly, and I remember trying to sleep with these horrible curlers in my hair. . . .

[Then at college] I was really ambivalent about it [all] because I still liked it, but you did not wear make-up, you did not dye your hair, you didn't wear a bra – we were all natural. Don't shave or anything. In some of the really early work, you can see my hairy legs. . . .

I hardly wear [make-up] in the day now . . . wearing make-up in daylight makes me look older. But at night, when the lights are low, I feel I can get away with it.

Cindy Sherman

When I want the entire love of one good man – the one I'm married to – I don't use it, but when I'm not so single-minded, out comes the old lipstick.

Woman and Beauty (1931)

A term coined by Leonard Lauder in 2001, the 'lipstick effect' refers to the financial phenomenon whereby sales of such small cosmetic indulgences go shooting up as the economy plummets into the red. It was therefore an intriguing reflection of post-Brexit-vote uncertainty that in the three months after Britain elected to leave the European Union, UK sales of lipstick outperformed an already flourishing cosmetic category by 30 per cent, echoing the 25 per cent surge seen during the Great Depression. The apparent paradox is easily explained; for not only is lipstick a cost-effective touch of luxury, it can also provide much-needed confidence when facing up to difficult times. As one World War II cosmetic ad declared: 'No lipstick – ours or anyone else's – will win the war. But it symbolises one of the reasons why we are fighting.'

Katy Young

Beauty is often spoken of as though it only stirs lust or admiration, but the most beautiful people are so in a way that makes them look like destiny or fate or meaning, the heroes of a remarkable story. Desire for them is in part a desire for a noble destiny, and beauty can seem like a door to meaning as well as to pleasure. And yet such people are often nothing extraordinary except for their effect on others. Exceptional beauty and charm are among those gifts given by the sinister fairy at the christening. They give the bearer considerable sway over others, which can keep them so busy being a siren on the rocks where others shipwreck that they forget that they themselves need to figure out where they are going.

Rebecca Solnit

Love built on beauty, soon as beauty, dies.
John Donne

Grey is obviously something most women on TV don't do but I think most people tuned into *Meet the Romans* because they wanted to learn about the Romans. And what I had to say was important. Grey is my hair colour. I really can't see why I should change it. There clearly is a view of female normative beauty but more women of 58 do look like me than like Victoria Beckham.
Mary Beard

Before you get dressed, you gotta know what your best assets are and how to play them to the hilt. This has to do with your outward, obvious physical pluses, of course, but more importantly, your inner feelings about sensuous style.

Chances are, you already know what your unique and finest physical assets are. You also know, having developed an appreciation for your U-world, how lingerie can serve where nature may have been a little lax, improving any aspect of your anatomy and making every part of you breathtaking. So working your assets off is about how clothes fit your psyche as much as how they fit your figure.

I know that snug, form-fitting clothes are best for me. Maybe the Empire-waist dress with mile-long sleeves is the ruling rage. I don't care. Sure, some babes look delectable in those swingy little trapeze dresses. But that's simply not my style. I know that I can best realize my Goddess Complex in clothes that cling to my every curve because of the way they make *me* feel. But, within the spectrum of snug, there's a whole lot of variety that can superbly suit all facets of my style personality. Because every babe has a 'multiple-style personality'.

Style is constantly reinventing yourself. With clothes, makeup, hairstyles, you bring out different aspects of you – the you of the moment. And, babe, you'd be surprised how many women you are! Everything from sweet, darling, adorable angel baby to vixen, villainess, diablesse, and every babe in between – they are alive inside you!

Most of the time you're an irresistible combination of angelic and devilish. Maybe one day you feel a little naughtier; the next, the scales tip toward the sweetness side. Every day, before you put on a stitch of clothing, think about the dramatic duality of your nature and the incredible range in between. Figure out how you feel today and dress the part! You are every woman in one woman and need a full spectrum of style.

Rose Miyonga It's been over three years since I stopped wearing make-up regularly. I still wear it sometimes for the odd photo shoot, or, if the mood strikes me, I might brush a little glitter over my eyelids or slick on a bit of lipstick, but day-to-day, I don't wear make-up.

Don't get me wrong, I think make-up is awesome.

When it's done by someone skilled, it is a true art. However, I apparently lack the motor skills needed to apply it properly, and my daily attempts at it often drove me to frustration and despair, and sometimes inflicted physical pain – I can't be the only one who has poked their still-sleepy eye with a mascara brush in the morning.

I have been asked so many times why I have chosen to opt out as if not wearing make-up is something so unnatural. The answer is pretty simple: for the moment, I just prefer being bare-faced.

As a woman, and especially a woman of colour, my body is too often the battleground on which issues of gender and race are fought, and the use of make-up is a prime example. It is as though I am denied the freedom to let my personal choice be just that: personal. It is so often assumed that my decision not to wear make-up is a 'stand' that I am taking for my intersectional feminist agenda, but it is not.

Sure, I do reject the idea of policing of women's bodies and telling them how they should or shouldn't look. I was lucky enough to grow up in a family where I was taught to question preconceived ideas of what it means to be a beautiful woman, and learned to look at my face in the mirror with love and acceptance. This, for me, right now, doesn't involve make-up every day. . . .

I choose not to wear make-up (or sometimes to do so) because I hope that I am part of the first generation of women of colour whose personal choices do not have to be held up to a political ideal, but can instead follow whims, moods and fancies without judgement or moralisation.

If you have been a beauty, ageing must be intolerable. . . . The process is bad enough as it is – the ebbing away of possibilities, the awful tyranny of the body – but for those who lose their very trade mark, it is savage.

Penelope Lively

Barbie's disfigured. It's fine to play with her just as long as you keep that in mind.

Lena Dunham

Lipstick colour – the options are endless. Some people have their signature shade – like my friend Polly who rocked Rimmel's 'Heather Shimmer' all through Uni. The irridescent mauve colour was as much 'her' as her ringlets, smile, friendship. Eve Ensler – that RED mouth – giving added power to the final 'CUNT!' of her one woman show *The Vagina Monologues.*

I noticed at this year's launch of One Billion Rising in NYC, that Eve replaced her signature red mouth with *silver.* We all approved, and interpreted the move like we were reading poetry. Which we were.

MAKE UP is SYMBOLISM. No matter how cheap, disposable, You Tubeable, fashionable, marketable, forgettable . . . Make Up marks us – and for that reason, it matters. We make it matter.

At the recent premiere of *Mad Max: Fury Road* here in LA I opted for a pale mouth and oily dark eyes.

Pale Lips are a statement. A colourless statement, but a statement. They say effortless. They say look at my eyes. *A bitten, berry shade lip is sexual; a pale lip is cerebral.* They have the wan look of 'I don't care', 'I'm not afraid' and 'I'm not trying to make you look at me (but I notice that you are)'. No wonder all the vampires are bloodless right down to the lip line. It's very cool, confident, modern – and if you take the vampire metaphor, it's immortal . . .

It's not as simple as wearing no lip colour – because we all have lip colour. We need to cover up the lip colour and replace it with something opaque. I quite like using foundation over my lips and then adding a hint of whatever cheek stain I've got going on.

Thandie Newton

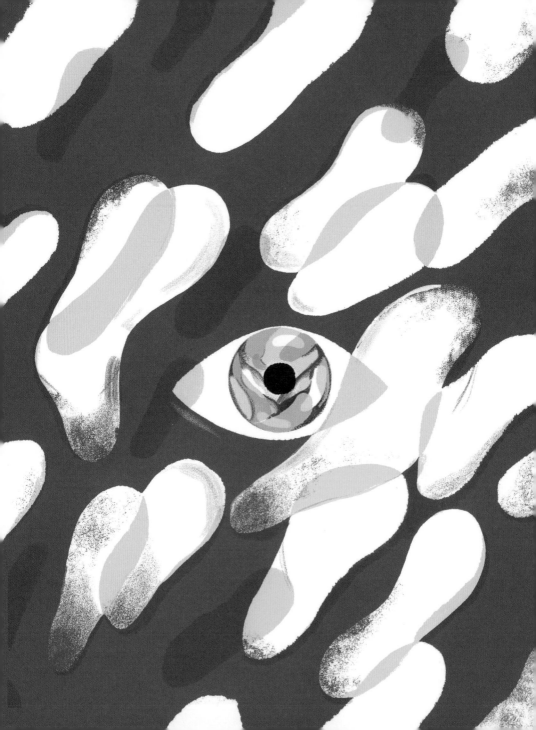

I think, then, that the beauty of the eye consists, first, in its *clearness*; what *coloured* eye shall please most, depends a good deal on particular fancies; but none are pleased with an eye whose water (to use that term) is dull and muddy. We are pleased with the eye in this view, on the principle upon which we like diamonds, clear water, glass, and such like transparent substances. Secondly, the motion of the eye contributes to its beauty, by continually shifting its direction; but a slow and languid motion is more beautiful than a brisk one; the latter is enlivening; the former lovely. Thirdly, with regard to the union of the eye with the neighboring parts, it is to hold the same rule that is given of other beautiful ones; it is not to make a strong deviation from the line of the neighboring parts; nor to verge into any exact geometrical figure. Besides all this, the eye affects, as it is expressive of some qualities of the mind, and its principal power generally arises from this.

Edmund Burke

While roses are so red,
     While lilies are so white,
Shall a woman exalt her face
     Because it gives delight?
She's not so sweet as a rose,
     A lily's straighter than she,
And if she were as red or white,
     She'd be but one of three.

Whether she flush in love's summer,
     Or in its winter grow pale,
Whether she flaunt her beauty
     Or hide it away in a veil;
Be she red or white,
     And stand she erect or bowed,
Time will win the race he runs with her
     And hide her away in a shroud.

Christina Rossetti

A woman may possess the wisdom and chastity of Minerva, and we give no heed to her, if she has a plain face. What folly will not a pair of bright eyes make pardonable? What dullness may not red lips are sweet accents render pleasant?

William Makepeace Thackeray

1951 Kerstin Håkansson, Sweden
Originally called the Festival Bikini contest and part of the 1951 Festival of Britain, the beauty pageant created by Eric Morley (Public Relations Officer of festival organizers Mecca, Ltd.) attracted so much publicity that it soon became known as 'Miss World' by the international press, prompting Morley to trademark the title. Håkansson would, in fact, be the only winner in a bikini as future competitions switched to the one-piece bathing suit. Morley said some years later that Håkansson 'filled a bikini more perfectly than anyone I have seen, before or since, and among all the Miss World winners she ranks as just about the most delectable'. She received a cheque for £1,000 and a pearl necklace.

1968 Penelope Plummer, Australia
Miss Philippines, Cecilia Amabuyok, was a novice Roman Catholic nun. At a banquet given before the Miss World contest at Britain's Variety Club, the men wolf-whistled, stamped their feet, and hoisted her onto a table. She finished in fourth place. Spain's Maria Amparo Rodrigo Lorenza walked out the night before the finals when Miss Gibraltar refused

to apologize for saying that she was glad Miss Spain was in the contest. Spain had declined to participate in Miss World for several years due to the presence of Miss Gibraltar. On the same evening as Miss Spain's withdrawal, Lebanon's Lili Bissar was disqualified after it was discovered she was only fifteen years old.

1982 Mariasela Álvarez, Dominican Republic
Miss Bermuda, Heather Ross, was charged with illegally importing cocaine valued at £200,000 into Britain. She was arrested at Heathrow Airport after stepping off a plane from Amsterdam, nine days into the Miss World contest in which she was unplaced. She served thirteen months of a three-year sentence. Of the winner, Miss Germany, Kerstin Paeserack, remarked, 'They might as well rename the contest Miss Virgin World. All they want is a safe little virgin who will trot around visiting hospitals for them. And that is what they got. It was a farce.' Miss Italy, Raffaella del Rosario, offered, 'There is something strange about her face. Her mouth is too big, and her chin sticks out.'

1996 Irene Skliva, Greece
Concerned at the apparent commodification of the female form and

the undermining of Indian culture, the contest – held in Bangalore, India – was marred by ongoing violent protests. One man committed suicide by setting himself on fire. Five days before the contest, protestors including activists of the All India Women's Democratic Association (AIDWA) were beaten by police during a demonstration, with at least four hundred being detained until the evening. Police swung bamboo canes, fired rubber bullets and launched tear gas at the protestors. Members of the forum for awakening women threatened its members would mingle with spectators and immolate themselves after taking poison. The protesters argued that the contest benefitted only plastic surgeons and cosmetics manufacturers. Its TV audience for this year was one of the highest ever, at 2.2 billion viewers worldwide.

2000 Priyanka Chopra, India

Organizer Eric Morley died at the beginning of November, weeks before the contest. His wife and co-organizer, Julia Morley, took control of the event and one of her first tasks after the title was awarded to Miss India was to issue the statement, 'There is no fixing in the Miss World Beauty Contest'. This was because of intense media speculation at the time over the dominance of India in the contest in recent years and the surge of multinational companies investing in the region. In the final round of questioning Chopra had been asked to name the living woman she admired most. She answered 'Mother Teresa', who had been dead for three years. The answer won her the crown but increased speculation of contest-rigging. Justifying her answer, Chopra, who had previously revealed that she wanted to be a clinical psychologist so as 'to understand why people turn demented', said, 'For me she is a living legend. She does live on for me.'

2005 Unnur Birna Vilhjálmsdóttir, Iceland

The Miss World 1983 finalist, Unnur Steinsson of Iceland was three months pregnant during the pageant. This violated the pageant's rules and ordinarily warranted disqualification; however, it wasn't discovered until after the pageant. Her baby, born on 25 May 1984, was the 2005 winner.

A beautiful face is a silent commendation.

Francis Bacon

A French writer asserts that the style of a woman's dress must depend upon the shape of her nose! If she has a prominent, strongly-marked nose she must dress either with great richness or great severity; if she has a retrousse or irregular nose, a piquant, coquettish costume will be in keeping; while for the great majority with noses of no shape in particular a style of simple quiet elegance is *de rigueur.*

I see good grooming and feminism as entirely complementary. For some, beauty is a matter of pride and self-respect, of feeling your best and worthy of attention. While a man with an interest in football, wine, Formula 1 or even paintballing would never see his intelligence called into question, a woman with an interest in surface is perceived to have no depth. I believe it's perfectly normal to love both lipstick and literature, to be a woman who paints her nails while shouting at *Question Time.*

Sali Hughes

Sources

p. 4 Margaret Wolfe Hungerford, *Molly Bawn* (Bel Air, Dodo Press, 2008)

Defining Beauty

p. 10 *Concise Oxford English Dictionary*, 12th edition, edited by Angus Stevenson and Maurice Waite (Oxford, Oxford University Press, 2011)

p. 11 Grace Nichols, 'Beauty', *The Fat Back Woman's Poems* (London, Virago, 1984)

p. 12 Andy Warhol, *The Philosophy of Andy Warhol (From A to B and Back Again)* (New York City, Harcourt Publishers Ltd, 1977)

p. 14 Emily Dickinson, 'I Died for Beauty', *The Poems of Emily Dickinson, edited by R.W. Franklin* (Harvard University Press, 1999)

p. 16 John Keats, 'Endymion', *John Keats: The Complete Poems* (London, Penguin Classics, 1977)

Tina Fey, *Bossypants* (London, Sphere, 2011)

p. 17 Marilynne Robinson, 'On "Beauty"', *The World Split Open: Great Authors on How and Why We Write* (Portland, Tin House Books, 2014)

p. 18 William Hogarth, *The Analysis of Beauty* (London, printed by John Reeves for the author, 1753)

p. 20 Aristotle, *Metaphysics* (Volume 2), (Cambridge, Harvard University Press, 1935)

Immanuel Kant, *The Critique of Judgement* (Indianapolis, Hackett Publishing, 1987)

p. 21 Marcus Aurelius, *Meditations* (London, Penguin, 2006)

p. 23 Richard Feynman, 'The Beauty of a Flower', recording from BBC *Horizon: 1981–1982, The Pleasure of Finding Things Out*

p. 24 Autumn Whitefield-Madrano, *Face Value: The Hidden Ways Beauty Shapes Women's Lives* (New York, Simon & Schuster, 2016)

p. 28 Anjan Chatterjee, quoted in 'Beauty: is it really only skin deep?' by Caroline Schmitt, *DW* (27 February 2015) http://p.dw.com/p/1EiIC

p. 30 Fyodor Dostoevsky, *The Brothers Karamazov*, translated by Constant Garnett (London, Heinemann, 1912)

p. 31 Edmund Burke, *On Taste, On the Sublime and Beautiful, Reflections on the French Revolution & A Letter to a Nobile Lord* (New York, Cosimo Classics, 2009)

p. 32 Baruch Spinoza, quoted in Fredrick Pollock, *Spinoza: His Life and Philosophy*, 2nd edition, (New York, American Scholar Publications, 1899)

p. 33 George Santayana, *The Sense of Beauty* (Mineola, Dover Publications Inc., 1955)

p. 34 William Butler Yeats, 'The Old Men Admiring Themselves in the Water', in *The Collected Poems of W.B. Yeats* (Ware, Wordsworth Editions, 2000).

p. 35 Wendy Steiner, *Venus in Exile* (Chicago, University of Chicago Press, 2001)

p. 37 Elaine Scarry, *On Beauty and Being Just* (London, Gerald Duckworth & Co. Ltd, 2000)

p. 40 Phuntsok Drolma, translated by Séagh Kehoe, in 'Plateau Redness and the Politics of Beauty in Contemporary Tibet' (24 March 2016): https://seaghkehoe.com/2016/03/24/the-politics-of-plateau-redness-part-1

p. 42 Johann Wolfgang Von Goethe in *Conversations of Goethe* by Johann Peter Eckermann, (Boston, DaCappo Press, 1998)

p. 43 Oscar Wilde, *The Picture of Dorian Gray*, (London, Penguin, 2003)

p. 44 Roxie Jane Hunt, '2015 Beauty Takeback: Feminism and the Beauty Industry', *Huffington Post* (13 March, 2015): https://www.huffingtonpost.com/roxie-jane-hunt/2015-beauty-takeback-feminism-and-the-beauty-industry_b_6850318.html

p. 46 Pablo Picasso, quoted in Jaime Sabartés, *Picasso: An Intimate Portrait* (London, W.H. Allen, 1949)

p. 47 Khalil Gibran, 'Beauty', *The Prophet* (New York, Alfred A. Knopf, 1923)

p. 48 Mary Wollstonecraft, *A Vindication of the Rights of Woman*, (London, Penguin, 2004)

p. 50 William Blake, *The Marriage of Heaven and Hell*, facsimile edition (Mineola, Dover Publications Inc., 2000)

p. 51 Arabelle Sicardi, 'Beauty Is Broken', *The Men Issue* (10 December 2015): https://medium.com/matter/beauty-is-broken-62dfd2be69df

p. 52 John Galsworthy, *The Forsyte Saga* (London, Heinemann, 1906–1921)

p. 53 Eric Jarosinski, quoted in 'Beauty: is it really only skin deep?' by Caroline Schmitt, *DW* (27 February 2015) http://p.dw.com/p/1EiIC

Voltaire, 'Beautiful, Beauty', from *A Pocket Philosophical Dictionary*, translated by John Fletcher (Oxford, Oxford University Press, 2011)

Finding Beauty

p. 56 Northrop Frye, 'Ethical Criticism: Theory of Symbols', *The Anatomy of Criticism* (Princeton, Princton University Press, 1957)

p. 57 Paige Brown Jarreau, 'Do you see Beauty in Nature? You may be more Satisfied with Life', *From the Lab Bench* (16 June 2014): http://www.fromthelabbench.com/from-the-lab-bench-science-blog/do-you-see-beauty-in-nature-you-may-be-more-satisfied-with-life

Saul Bellow, *Herzog* (London, Penguin Classics, 2001)

p. 58 Steve Biko, *I Write What I Like: a selection of his writings* edited by Aelred Stubbs CR (Oxford, Heinemann Educational Publishers, 1987)

John Cage, quoted on *American Masters John Cage: I Have Nothing to Say and I Am Saying It* (PBS, 1990). VHS.

p. 59 William Shakespeare, 'Sonnet 130', in *The Complete Works of William Shakespeare* (Ware, Wordsworth Editions, 1996)

p. 60 Lupita Nyong'o, speech at the Essence Black Women in Hollywood luncheon, 2014

p. 61 William Morris, quoted in Jan Marsh, *William Morris and Red House* (London, National Trust Books, 2005)

p. 63 Hafsa Issa-Salwe, 'Exploring my Heritage through Beauty', *Muslimah Beauty* (18 February 2016): http://muslimahbeauty.com/2016/02/18/exploring-my-heritage-through-beauty/

p. 65 David Hume, 'Essay XXIII: Of the Standard of Taste', *Essays, Moral, Political and Literary (1742)*, edited by Eugene F Miller (Indianapolis, Liberty Fund Inc., 1987)

p. 66 Joseph Addison, 'Pleasures of the Imagination', *Spectator* No. 412 (23 June 1712)

p. 67 French proverb

p. 68 Marcel Proust, *Remembrance of Things Past: Swann's Way*, translated by C.K. Scott Moncrieff (London, Vintage, 1996)

p. 71 John O'Donohue, *Beauty: The Invisible Embrace*, (London, Harper Perennial, 2005)

p. 72 Joan Collins, interviewed by Lynnette Peck, 'Joan Collins' Beauty Secrets', *Saga*: https://www.saga.co.uk/magazine/style-beauty/beauty/joan-collins-beauty-secrets

Marshall McLuhan, 'Fashion is Language: McLuhan's Bazaar,' *Harper's Bazaar* (April 1968)

p. 73 Luciana Avedon *née* Pignatelli, *The Beautiful People's Beauty Book*, as told to Jeanne Molli (London, W.H. Allen, 1971)

p. 74 Geoffrey Chaucer, 'Rondel of Merciless Beauty', *All Poetry*: https://allpoetry.com/Rondel-of-Merciless-Beauty

p. 75 Friedrich Schiller, 'Letter XVIII', 'Letters Upon the Aesthetical Education of Man', from *Literary and Philosophical Essays* (Harvard, Harvard Classics, 1909–14)

Scarlett Johansson, *Seventeen* magazine (May 2007)

p. 76 Naomi Wolf, *The Beauty Myth* (London, Vintage, 1991)

p. 78 Havelock Ellis, *On Life and Sex: Essays of Love & Virtue* (London, Butterworth-Heinemann, 2013)

p. 79 Kate Moss, interviewed by Sonia Haria, *Stella* magazine (19 July 2015)

p. 80 Larissa Vingilis-Jaremko, quoted in 'Beauty: is it really only skin deep?' by Caroline Schmitt, *DW* (27 February 2015) http://p.dw.com/p/1EiIC

p. 81 Mark Tungate, *Branded Beauty* (London, Kogan Page Limited, 2011)

p. 82 Lisa Ferber, interviewed by Autumn Whitefield-Madran, *The Beheld* (23 March 2011): http://www.the-beheld.com/2011/03/lisa-ferber-artist-new-york-city.html

p. 85 Simone de Beauvoir, *The Second Sex*, translated by Constance Borde and Shelia Malovany-Chevallier (London, Vintage Classics, 1997)

p. 86 Rachel Carson, *The Sense of Wonder*, (New York, Harper Collins, 1997)

Sources

p. 87 Charles Dickens, *The Mystery of Edwin Drood* (Ware, Wordsworth Editions, 2005)

p. 88 Marcelo Gleiser, *The Simple Beauty of the Unexpected* (Lebanon, ForeEdge, 2016)

p. 89 'A Professional Beauty', *Beauty and How to Keep It* (London, Brentano's, 1889)

p. 90 Adele Waldman, '"A First-rate Girl": The Problem of Female Beauty', *The New Yorker* (2 October 2013)

p. 91 Virginia Woolf, 'Street Haunting', *Street Haunting and Other Essays* (London, Vintage Classics, 2014)

p. 92 Ralph Waldo Emerson, quoted in *A Dictionary of Thoughts*, edited by Tryon Edwards (Detroit, F.B. Dickerson Co, 1908)

p. 94 Blaise Pascal, *Pensées* (London, Penguin Classics, 1995)

p. 96 Roger Scruton, *Beauty* (Oxford, Oxford University Press, 2009)

p. 97 Ruth Fainlight, 'Friends' Photos', in *New and Collected Poems* (London, Bloodaxe Books, 2010)

p. 98 David McRaney, *You Can Beat Your Brain* (London, Oneworld, 2013)

p. 100 Plato, *Symposium (Oxford World's Classics)* (Oxford, Oxford University Press, 2008)

p. 101 Alexander Pope, *The Poetical Works of Alexander Pope*, edited by the Rev. H.F. Cary (London, William Smith, 1841)

Living Beautifully

p. 104 William Morris, 'The Beauty of Life', *Hopes and Fears for Art: Five Lectures Delivered in Birmingham, London, and Nottingham, 1878–1881* (London, Ellis & White, 1882)

p. 105 Katharine Mansfield, 'Bliss', in *The Collected Stories of Katharine Mansfield* (Ware, Wordsworth Editions, 2006)

Lauren Bacall, as quoted in the *Daily Telegraph* (2 March 1988)

p. 106 Friedrich Nietzsche, *The Gay Science*, (New York, Random House USA, 1991)

Kathleen Marie Higgins 'Whatever Happened to Beauty? A Response to Danto', *Beauty* (London, Whitechapel Gallery, 2009)

p. 107 Buddha, *Dhammapada* 262-3, translated by Narada Thera (London, John Murray, 1959)

p. 108 Nadine Gordimer, 'Leaving School – II', *London* magazine (May 1963)

Ellen Sturgis Hooper, 'I Slept, and Dreamed that Life Was Beauty', in *The Transcendentalists: An Anthology*, edited by Perry Miller (Harvard, Harvard University Press, 1950)

p. 109 Arthur C. Danto, *The Abuse of Beauty: Aesthetics and the Concept of Art* (Chicago, Open Court, 2003)

p. 110 Erich Fromm, *The Art of Loving* (London, Thorsons, 1995)

p. 112 Brigitte Bardot, quoted in the *Chicago Tribune*, 7 July 1987

Psalm 16:11, Holy Bible (The Voice translation, 2012)

p. 113 Jane Austen, *Northanger Abbey* (London, Vintage Classics, 2014)

p. 114 Bertrand Russell, *What I Believe*, (London, Routledge, 2004)

Alice Walker, '"Democratic Womanism": Poet and Activist on Women Rising, Obama and the 2012 Election', interview with Amy Goodman for *Democracy Now!* (28 September 2012): https://www.democracynow.org/2012/9/28/democratic_womanism_poet_and_activist_alice

p. 115 Augustine of Hippo, 'Homilies on the First Epistle of John', *The Works of Saint Augustine*, Vol. 1 (New York, New City Press, 2008)

p. 116 Damon Young, *Distraction*, (Durham, Acumen Publishing Ltd, 2010)

p. 117 Percy Bysshe Shelley, *Prometheus Unbound*, (London, C&J Ollier, 1820)

Jesinta Campbell, *Live A Beautiful Life* (Sydney, Hachette Australia, 2016)

p. 119 Anaïs Nin, as quoted by Carol A. Dingle in *French Writers of the Past* (Indiana, iUniverse, 2000)

p. 120 Caitlin Moran, interviewed in *Stylist* magazine (June 2011)

p. 121 Diana Vreeland, quoted in *Cheap Chic* by Caterine Milinaire and Carol Troy (London, Omnibus Press, 1975)

p. 122 Anne Brontë, *The Tenant of Wildfell Hall* (Ware, Wordsworth Editions, 1996)

p. 123 Marie Kondo, *The Life-Changing Magic of Tidying Up* (London, Vermilion, 2014)

p. 124 Chimamanda Ngozi Adichie, interview with Susan Riley, *Stylist* (21 March 2017): https://www.stylist.co.uk/people/chimamanda-ngozi-adichie-interview-author-we-should-all-be-feminists-half-of-a-yellow-son/32944

p. 125 Simone Weil, *Simone Weil: An Anthology*, edited by Sian Miles (London, Penguin Classics, 2005)

p. 126 Edith Wharton, quoted by Hermione Lee in *Edith Wharton* (London, Chatto & Windus, 2007)

p. 128 Pema Chödrön, *Living Beautifully* (Mount Pocono, Shambhala, 2012)

p. 129 Harmony Korine, *Gummo*, Dir. Harmony Korine (Fine Line Features, 1997). DVD.

Helen Gurley Brown, *Having It All* (London, Sidgwick & Jackson, 1983)

p. 130 Lynne Segal, *Out of Time: the pleasures and perils of aging* (London, Verso, 2013)

p. 132 Michael Zadoorian, *The Leisure Seeker* (London, Harper, 2018)

p.133 D.H. Lawrence, *A Modern Lover and Other Writings* (Oxford, Oxford University Press 1995)

Arundhati Roy, *The Cost of Living* (New York, Modern Library, 1999)

p. 135 Yves Saint Laurent, quoted by Alice Cavanagh in 'Yves Saint Lauren Celebrates 50 Years in the Beauty Business', *The Australian* (6 June 2014)

p. 136 Coco Chanel, quoted by *Marie Claire* (4 October 2016): http://www.marieclaire.co.uk/fashion/coco-chanel-s-25-snappiest-quotes-54026

p. 137 Rabindranath Tagore, *Stray Birds* (India, Macmillan India, 1978)

Peter Ilich Tchaikovsky, *Life and Letters of Peter Ilich Tchaikovsky*, edited by Modeste Tchaikovsky (Honolulu, University Press of the Pacific, 2004

p. 138 Albert Einstein, quoted in *Albert Einstein, The Human Side: Glimpses from his Archives*, edited by Helen Dukas and Banesh Hoffman (Princeton, Princeton University Press, 2013)

p. 139 Wendell Berry, *What Are People For?* (Berkeley, Counterpoint, 2010)

p. 140 Robyn Griggs Lawrence, 'Wabi-Sabi: The Art of Imperfection', *Utne Reader* (September–October 2001): http://www.utne.com/mind-and-body/wabi-sabi

p.142 Amit Ray, *Nonviolence: The Transforming Power* (Swarg Ashram, Inner Light Publishers, 2012)

p. 143 Friedrich Nietzsche, *Thus Spoke Zarathustra* (Ware, Wordsworth Editions, 1997)

Willa Cather, *The Selected Letters of Willa Cather*, edited by Andrew Jewell (New York Knopf, 2013)

p. 144 Sam Levenson, *In One Era and Out the Other* (New York, Pocket Books, 1974)

p. 145 Yann Martel, *Life of Pi*, (Edinburgh, Canongate Books, 2012)

p. 146 Caroline Schmitt, '8 Steps to Inner Beauty', *DW* (12 March 2015): http://p.dw.com/p/1Ep55

p. 147 Karen Armstrong, *Twelve Steps To A Compassionate Life* (New York, Knopf, 2010)

p. 148 Cheryl Strayed, *Tiny Beautiful Things: Advice on Love and Life from Dear Sugar* (New York, Vintage Books, 2012)

p. 149 Orhan Pamuk, *The New Life* (London, Faber & Faber, 2015)

Leon Trotsky, 'On Optimism and Pessimism, on the Twentieth Century, and on Many Other Things' (1901), as quoted in *The Prophet Armed: Trotsky, 1879–1921* (2003) by Isaac Deutscher (London, Verso, 2003)

Inner Beauty

p. 152 Charlotte Brontë, *Jane Eyre* (London, Penguin Classics, 2012)

p. 153 Plato, *Phaedrus (Oxford World's Classics)* (Oxford, Oxford University Press, 2009)

Roald Dahl, *The Twits* (London, Puffin, 2013)

p. 154 Elizabeth Taylor, *Elizabeth Takes Off* (New York, Putnam Group, 1988)

p. 155 Francis Bacon, 'Of Beauty', from *The Essays or Counsels, Civil and Moral* (Oxford, Oxford World Classics, 1999)

Sources

p. 156 Morihei Ueshiba, *The Art of Peace* (Mount Pocono, Shambhala Publications, 2010)

p. 157 1 Peter 3:3–4, Holy Bible (NIV, 2011)

p. 158 Joan Collins, *The Joan Collins Beauty Book* (London, Macmillan, 1980)

p. 160 Friedrich Schiller, quoted in 'An Unfamiliar and Positive Law: On Kant and Schiller', by Reed Winegar, *Archiv für Geschichte der Philosophie*, 95(3), (2013)

p. 161 William Shakespeare, 'Sonnet 18', in *The Complete Works of William Shakespeare* (Ware, Wordsworth Editions, 1996)

p. 162 Drew Barrymore, quoted by Rick Porter in 'Drew Barrymore on "having it all": "I don't. I can't"', *Screener* (6 April 2013): http://screenertv.com/news-features/drew-barrymore-on-having-it-all-i-dont-i-cant

Ruby Dee, quoted by Glenda Dickerson in *African American Theatre: A Cultural Companion* (Cambridge, Polity, 2008)

p. 163 Ralph Waldo Emerson, *The Complete Works of Ralph Waldo Emerson: The Conduct of Life* (Vol. 6), (Boston; New York, Houghton Mifflin, 1903–4)

p. 164 Carina Tyrrell, quoted by Adrian Lee in 'Cambridge Medical Student Claims She Is Feminist after Winning Miss England', *Daily Express* (19 June 2014)

p. 165 Helen Keller, *The Story of My Life by Helen Keller* (New York, Grosset & Dunlap, 1905)

p. 167 Elizabeth Kübler-Ross *Death: The Final Stage of Growth* (New York, Simon & Schuster, 1997)

p. 168 Proverbs 27:19, Holy Bible (NIV, 2011)

Frances Hodgson Burnett, *A Little Princess* (London, Puffin Classics, 2014)

p. 169 Amy Randall, 'Young Feminist: Fitting into Jeans, or Fitting into Society?', *National Women's Health Network* (14 March 2016): https://www.nwhn.org/young-feminist-fitting-into-jeans-or-fitting-into-society/

p. 170 *Beauty for Every Woman* (London, The Syndicate Publishing Company, 1930)

p. 172 Ursula K. Le Guin, *The Wave in the Mind* (Boulder, Shambala Publications, 2004)

p. 174 Mark Vernon, *Use Philosophy to be Happier: 30 Steps to Perfect the Art of Living* (Boston, Teach Yourself, 2013)

p. 175 Dave Eggers, *A Heartbreaking Work of Staggering Genius* (London, Picador, 2007)

Carol Morgan, 'Outer Beauty vs. Inner Beauty: We Have it Backwards', *Huffington Post* (1 April 2017): https://www.huffingtonpost.com/dr-carol-morgan/outer-beauty-vs-inner-bea_b_9585726.html

p. 176 Plotinus, *Ennead V, The Complete Works of Plotinus*, translated by Stephen MacKenna (Delphi Classics, 2015)

p. 178 Marcus Aurelius, *Meditations* (New York, Modern Library, 2003)

Walter Mosley, *The Last Days of Ptolemy Gray* (New York, Riverhead Books, 2010)

p. 179 George Eliot (Mary Anne Shaw), *Adam Bede* (London, Penguin, 2008)

p. 181 Maurice Materlinck, 'The Inner Beauty', in *A Library of the World's Best Literature*, Vol. XXIV, edited by Charles Dudley Warner (New York, Cosimo Classics, 2008)

p. 182 Erin Tatum, 'Don't Call Me Beautiful (And What to Say Instead)', *Everyday Feminism* (17 June 2014): https://everydayfeminism.com/2014/06/dont-call-me-beautiful

p. 184 Vivian Diller, quoted in 'Beauty: is it really only skin deep?' by Caroline Schmitt, *DW* (27 February 2015) http://p.dw.com/p/1EiIC

p. 185 Kate Winslet, 'Kate Winslet Looks Ahead', interview with Laura Brown, *Harper's Bazaar* (8 July 2009): http://www.harpersbazaar.com/celebrity/latest/news/a398/kate-winslet-0809/

p. 186 Tobias Hürter, quoted in 'Beauty: is it really only skin deep?' by Caroline Schmitt, *DW* (27 February 2015) http://p.dw.com/p/1EiIC

p. 188 Lillian Bradstock and Jane Condon, *The Modern Woman* (London, Associated Newspapers Ltd, 1936)

p. 190 Plutarch *Life of Anthony* edited by C B R Pelling (Cambridge, Cambridge University Press, 1988)

p. 191 Ellen DeGeneres, *Seriously . . . I'm Kidding* (New York, Grand Central Publishing, 2013)

Outer Beauty

p. 194 F. Scott Fitzgerald, *The Crack-up* edited by Edmund Wilson, (New York, New Directions, 2009)

Leo Tolstoy, *War and Peace* (London, Penguin, 1982)

p. 195 Gloria Steinem, *My Life on the Road* (London, Oneworld, 2015)

p. 196 Elizabeth Gaskell, *Wives and Daughters* (Ware, Wordsworth Editions, 1999)

George Bernard Shaw, as quoted in Mark Vernon, *Use Philosophy to be Happier: 30 Steps to Perfect the Art of Living* (Boston, Teach Yourself ,2013)

p. 197 Lord Byron, 'She Walks in Beauty' *Selected Poems* (London, Penguin Classics, 2005)

p. 198 Nancy Etcoff, *Survival of the Prettiest: The Science of Beauty* (New York, Anchor Books, 2000)

p. 200 Daniel S. Hamermesh, *Beauty Pays* (Princton, Princeton University Press, 2011)

p. 201 Luciana Avedon *née* Pignatelli, *The Beautiful People's Beauty Book*, as told to Jeanne Molli (London, W.H. Allen, 1971)

p. 202 Angela Carter, 'The Wound in the Face', *Nothing Sacred: Selected Writings* (London, Virago Press Ltd, 2016)

p. 205 Brothers Grimm (Jacob Grimm and Wilhelm Grimm), *Complete Fairytales of the Brothers Grimm* (Delphi Classics, 2017)

p. 207 Meryl Streep, quoted by Andrew Anthony in 'Super Trooper of the Silver Screen', *Guardian* (29 June 2008): https://www.theguardian.com/film/2008/jun/29/features.merylstreep

Anna Wintour, quoted in *The Presidential Campaign of Barack Obama: A Critical Analysis of a Racially Transcendent Strategy*, by Dewey M. Clayton (Abingdon, Routledge, 2010)

p. 208 Cindy Sherman, 'Me, Myself & I', interview with Simon Hattenstone, *Guardian* (15 January 2011): https://www.theguardian.com/artanddesign/2011/jan/15/cindy-sherman-interview

p. 209 *Woman and Beauty* magazine, 'The Lipstick Mood' by M. Banning (January 1931)

Katy Young, 'The Lipstick Index', *Harper's Bazaar* UK, (1 April 2017)

p. 210 Rebecca Solnit, *A Field Guide to Getting Lost* (New York, Penguin, 2006)

p. 212 John Donne, *Elegies*, No. 2 'The Anagram', in *John Donne: Collected Poetry* (London, Penguin Classics, 2012)

Mary Beard, 'Mary Beard: I almost didn't feel such generic, violent misogyny was about me', interview with Elizabeth Day, *Guardian* (26 January 2013): https://www.theguardian.com/books/2013/jan/26/mary-beard-question-time-internet-trolls

p. 213 Dianne Brill, *Boobs, Boys & High Heels* (London, Vermillion, 1992)

p. 214 Rose Miyonga, 'Make Up My Mind', *Thandie Kay* (28 November 2016): http://thandiekay.com/2016/11/28/22976

p. 216 Penelope Lively, *Spiderweb* (London, Penguin, 1999)

Lena Dunham, *Not That Kind of Girl* (London, Fourth Estate, 2014)

p. 217 Thandie Newton, 'Dark Skin Pale Lip', *Thandie Kay* (1 June 2015): http://thandiekay.com/2015/06/01/dark-skin-pale-lip

p. 219 Edmund Burke, *A Philosophical Enquiry into the Origin of Our Ideas of the Sublime and Beautiful* (Oxford, Oxford Paperbacks, 2008)

p. 220 Christina Rossetti, 'Beauty Is Vain', in *The Works of Christina Rossetti* (Ware, Wordsworth Editions, 1995)

p. 221 William Makepeace Thackeray, *Vanity Fair* (London, Penguin Classics, 1987)

p. 222 David Rose, *Sexually I'm More of a Switzerland: More Personal Ads from the London Review of Books* (London, Picador, 2011)

p. 224 Francis Bacon, *A Collection of Apothegms, New and Old by Francis Bacon, Baron of Verulum, Viscount St Alban*, (Oxford, Text Creation Partnerships, 2003)

p. 226 *Beauty: How to Get It and How to Keep It* (London, Tit-Bits Office, 1885)

p. 227 Sali Hughes, *Pretty Honest* (London, Fourth Estate, 2014)

Index of authors

Acknowledgements

Various publishers, individuals and estates have generously given permission to use extracts from the following copyright works.

Karen Armstrong, *Twelve Steps to a Compassionate Life*, copyright © 2010 by Karen Armstrong. Used by permission of Alfred A. Knopf, an imprint of the Knopf Doubleday Publishing Group, a division of Penguin Random House LLC. All rights reserved.

Simone de Beauvoir, *The Second Sex* translated by Constance Borde and Sheila Malovany-Chevallier, translation copyright © 2009 by Constance Borde and Sheila Malovany-Chevallier. Used by permission of Alfred A. Knopf, an imprint of the Knopf Doubleday Publishing Group, a division of Penguin Random House LLC. All rights reserved.

Saul Bellow, *Herzog* copyright © 1961, 1963, 1964, renewed 1989, 1991, 1992 by Saul Bellow. Used by permission of Viking Books, an imprint of Penguin Publishing Group, a division of Penguin Random House LLC. All rights reserved.

Wendell Berry, *What Are People For?* © 1990, 2010. Reprinted by permission of Counterpoint Press.

Steve Biko, *I Write What I Like* reproduced by permission of Bowerdean Press.

Helen Gurley Brown, *Having It All*, published by Hodder & Stoughton.

Jesinta Campbell, *Live a Beautiful Life* (2016) reproduced by permission of Hachette Australia.

Rachel Carson, *The Sense of Wonder* copyright © 1956 by Rachel Carson. Reprinted by permission of HarperCollins Publishers.

Angela Carter, 'The Wound in the Face', published by *New Society Magazine*, 1975. Copyright © Angela Carter. Reproduced by permission of the author c/o Rogers, Coleridge & White Ltd., 20 Powis Mews, London W11 1JN.

Willa Cather, *The Selected Letters of Willa Cather*, letters copyright © 2013 by The Willa Cather Literary Trust. Introduction, annotation, commentary and compilation copyright © 2013 by Andrew Jewell and Janis Stout. Used by permission of Alfred A. Knopf, an imprint of the Knopf Doubleday Publishing Group, a division of Penguin Random House LLC. All rights reserved.

Anjan Chatterjee, 'Beauty: is it really skin deep?' © Deutsche Welle.

Pema Chödrön, *Living Beautifully* reproduced by permission of the publisher, represented by The Permissions Company, Inc.

Roald Dahl, *The Twits*, text copyright © 1980 by Roald Dahl Nominee Limited. Used by permission of Alfred A. Knopf, an imprint of Random House Children's Books, a division of Penguin Random House LLC. All rights reserved. Reproduced by permission of David Higham Associates.

Ellen DeGeneres, *Seriously... I'm Kidding* reproduced by permission of Hachette/Grand Central Publishing.

Vivian Diller, 'Beauty: is it really skin deep?' © Deutsche Welle.

Lena Dunham, *Not That Kind of Girl*, copyright © 2014 by Lena Dunham. Used by permission of Random House, an imprint and division of Penguin Random House LLC. All rights reserved.

Dave Eggers, *A Heartbreaking Work of Staggering Genius* reproduced with permission of the Licensor through PLSclear.

Albert Einstein, republished with permission of Princeton University Press, from *Albert Einstein, The Human Side* edited by Helen Dukas and Banesh Hoffman, 2013; permission conveyed through Copyright Clearance Center, Inc.

Nancy Etcoff, *Survival of the Prettiest* copyright © 1999 by Nancy Etcoff. Used by permission of Doubleday, an imprint of the Knopf Doubleday Publishing Group, a division of Penguin Random House LLC. All rights reserved.

Ruth Fainlight, 'Friends' Photos' reproduced by permission of Bloodaxe Books.

Tina Fey, *Bossypants* reproduced by permission of Little, Brown Book Group Limited.

Richard Feynman, 'The Beauty of a Flower' © BBC.

Eric Fromm, *The Art of Loving* reprinted by permission of HarperCollins Publishers Ltd © 1995 Eric Fromm.

Northrop Frye, republished with permission of Princeton University Press, from *The Anatomy Criticism* by Northrop Frye, 1957; permission conveyed through Copyright Clearance Center, Inc.

Daniel S. Hamermesh, republished with permission of Princeton University Press, from *Beauty Pays* by Daniel S. Hamermesh, 2011; permission conveyed through Copyright Clearance Center, Inc.

Sali Hughes, *Pretty Honest* reprinted by permission of HarperCollins Publishers Ltd © 2014 Sali Hughes.

Tobias Hürter, 'Beauty: is it really skin deep?' © Deutsche Welle.

Hafsa Issa-Salwe, 'Exploring my Heritage through Beauty' reproduced by permission of the author.

Eric Jarosinski, 'Beauty: is it really skin deep?' © Deutsche Welle.

Marie Kondo, *The Life-Changing Magic of Tidying*, published by Vermilion. Reprinted by permission of The Random House Group Limited © 2014.

Elisabeth Kübler-Ross, *Death: The Final Stage of Growth*, copyright © 1975 by Elisabeth Kübler-Ross. Copyright renewed © 2003 by Elisabeth Kübler-Ross. Reprinted with the permission of Scribner, a division of Simon & Schuster, Inc. All rights reserved.

Robyn Griggs Lawrence, *Simply Imperfect: Revisiting the Wabi-Sabi House*, published by New Society Publishers, 2011. Reproduced by permission of the author.

Ursula Le Guin, *The Wave of the Mind* reproduced by permission of the publisher, represented by The Permissions Company, Inc.

Penelope Lively, *Spiderweb* reproduced by permission of David Higham Associates.

David McRaney, *You Can Beat Your Brain* reproduced with permission of the Licensor through PLSclear.

Thanks

I would like to thank everyone at White Lion Publishing for their tireless work in guiding this book from proposal to print, and especially Anna Watson for her many valuable suggestions. This book was only possible with the help of numerous writers, publishers, agents, executors and estates. Thank you all. A special thanks also goes to Emily Bick for sharing her incisive knowledge of beauty writing, and Jonathan Paul for support and beautiful cups of tea.

Selection and introduction © 2018 Helen Gordon
Illustrations © 2018 Amanda Berglund

This edition published in 2019 by Chartwell Books,
an imprint of The Quarto Group
142 West 36th Street, 4th Floor
New York, NY 10018 USA
T (212) 779-4972 **F** (212) 779-6058
www.QuartoKnows.com

First published in 2018 by White Lion Publishing,
an imprint of The Quarto Group.
The Old Brewery, 6 Blundell Street
London, N7 9BH, United Kingdom

Chartwell Books titles are also available at discount for retail, wholesale, promotional, and bulk purchase. For details,
contact the Special Sales Manager by email at specialsales@quarto.com or by mail at The Quarto Group, Attn: Special
Sales Manager, 100 Cummings Center Suite 265D, Beverly, MA 01915, USA.

10 9 8 7 6 5 4 3 2 1

ISBN: 978-0-7858-3807-4

Typeset in ITC New Baskerville
Design by Glenn Howard

Printed in China